Little Quilts

Sarah Fielke & Amy Lobsiger

Little Quilts

15 step-by-step
projects for adorably
small quilts

CICO BOOKS
LONDON NEW YORK

Published in 2014 by CICO Books
an imprint of Ryland Peters & Small
519 Broadway, 5th Floor, New York NY 10012
20–21 Jockey's Fields, London WC1R 4BW

www.rylandpeters.com

10 9 8 7 6 5 4 3 2 1

A CIP catalog record for this book is available from the
Library of Congress and the British Library.

ISBN: 978 1 78249 137 8

Printed in China

Copy editors: Erica Spinks and Alison Wormleighton
Designer: Geoff Borin
Photography: Sue Stubbs
Illustrations: Stephen Dew

All instructions in this book contain both standard
(imperial) and metric measurements. Please use only
one set of measurements when cutting out and
sewing as they are not interchangeable.

Contents

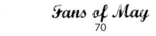

Introduction

The internet has had such an incredible impact on quilting. It has allowed the updated quilting bee, where quilters from across the globe come together in a virtual sense. They share their creations, sew along with others, and form online communities and friendships. Many of these relationships spill over into the "real" world as quilt guilds, sewing retreats, and even small businesses. To say that the internet has revolutionized quilting may be an exaggeration but it has extensively exposed quiltmaking to a new generation of sewers.

The virtual quilting world probably started as a Usenet newsgroup (a bulletin board type of communication network), more than a decade before the World Wide Web was developed. Rec.crafts.textiles.quilting was the Usenet group for quilters. Often, participants could be found at colleges and universities, as the computer network communications system was most common in academic environments. Quilters read messages posted to the group, replied, started new threads, "met," and often swapped fabrics or blocks through the mail. Compared with today, of course, it was a small group but it allowed sharing of quilting information to a worldwide audience.

Today, social media provides fabulous tools for quilters to share information, to show what they're working on, and to find others who share their tastes in fabrics and projects. We "gather" on Twitter, Facebook, Flickr, Pinterest, and Instagram. We buy and sell finished products and supplies on sites like Etsy. We take classes at Craftsy and Creativebug. We blog about our projects, our favorite fabrics, families, pets, and recipes.

The Doll Quilt Swap group on Flickr began in 2007. As of Spring 2014, the Flickr Doll Quilt Swap was on its fourteenth round of swapping small quilts between quilters all around the world. The impetus for this swap was a photograph of a wall of small quilts in a child's room shown in the book *Collecting American Country*. Blogger, author, and creator Hillary Lang posted the photograph that inspired her to make small quilts to decorate a wall in her daughter's nursery.

Doll quilts are wonderful projects for modern quilters. They can be completed relatively quickly and inexpensively, and then swapped, given away, or displayed on blogs. The blocks can be made into cushions, runners, or wall decorations, or used as lessons or for trialing larger projects.

With this in mind, take up your rotary cutter and begin! Each project in this book can be pieced, appliquéd, and quilted by hand or machine. Use the materials you have at hand to make them. The projects are wonderful for featuring the charm packs, jelly rolls, and fat-quarter bundles that we all have stashed away. The quilt backs can be made from fabrics left over from other projects and the batting (wadding) trimmed from the unused ends of larger quilts. Of course, there is nothing to stop you from buying all new fabrics for these little projects and stashing the rest!

When choosing fabrics to make these small quilts, keep in mind the scale of the pieces you will be cutting. If you are using scraps, make sure you have enough to cut all the pieces required. If you run short, though, don't be afraid to use two different fabrics combined for one specific place in the quilt. After all, these projects are supposed to be scrappy and fun, and also rather rustic.

In the spirit of international swapping and sharing of ideas and inspiration, we have started a Flickr group iat www.flickr.com/groups/littlequiltsbook/ and a Pinterest board at www.pinterest.com/LittleQuiltsBk/ so be sure to add photos of your creations and share them with others. We would love to hear about how you use this book, so let us know if you and your quilt group use our patterns to create quilts for each other.

Sarah and Amy

Amy

A shared love of cute and wee may have brought these quilts together, but it is probably truer that the stimulus was a bond formed by sarcasm. When we "met" online, Sarah was a widely known quilt teacher and co-owner of Material Obsession in Australia. I regularly stopped by the store's blog to admire and comment on happenings there. One year, shortly after I began my stalking, er, admiration, at the International Quilt Market in Houston, Texas, I saw a familiar face. It was Sarah Fielke! I fumbled, I broke into a sweat, I turned red, and then I spoke the famous words, "I read your blog." I could then say I knew Sarah in person! She was, of course, kind and gracious, accepting my ungraceful gushings.

Back online after that, I'm sure I sent a "remember me?" message. We would occasionally email back and forth, often with glib commentary on some subject. At one point, we discussed the utter cuteness that could be seen in so many of the doll quilts being swapped via Flickr.

"Have you seen?" "Can you stand it?" "Too cute for words!" "Squeeee!" We said: "What if we swap small quilts with each other?" This developed into: "What if we swap between ourselves and start a pattern subscription program for the quilts we swap?" Oh, yes, please! We started Dollies Online, mainly for the fun we had and our love of making teeny, tiny cute quilts. The program continued for two years with monthly offerings.

For me, the program was much more than making quilts and patterns. It saw me through some very difficult times and gave me a reason to focus on something other than life. So, importantly, it helped me celebrate a friendship, through thick and through thin. My respect and admiration for Sarah's talent, creativity, and skill continue to grow.

These little quilts showcase what we love most in small quilts, or what we call doll quilts. They are not miniature quilts in which an entire quilt is made to smaller proportions. We consider them akin to vintage doll quilts, perhaps made by a young girl as early needlework practice or perhaps made by a mother for her daughter's special doll. Sometimes these quilts are just one block or a few, but we like them to be special, whether by careful fabric combination or small details.

You will find that these quilts serve as guide and inspiration. There is nothing too daunting, but we have covered a lot of ground as far as techniques are concerned. You will find traditional piecing, English paper piecing, foundation piecing, hand appliqué, and embroidery. The quilts are not designed to be made in a hurry yet they are not intensely time-consuming because of their size. Perhaps they will give you a chance to try something new and find that you like it!

Sarah

My introduction to "doll quilts" came from a book on Amish quilting, many years ago—even before I owned a quilt shop. I am the sort of person who, on becoming interested in something, has to read everything about it that I can find. I have always read quilt books. I don't mean pattern books; I mean books about quilt history, and antique quilts, and quilters of the past. My library is vast and ever-growing.

In this beautiful old book there was a section on what they called doll quilts—essentially small quilts made by young girls for their dolls. These quilts were often the maker's first attempt at patchwork, and therefore quite simple and more than a little wonky. The quilts were made to be used in play, and so many have not survived the intervening years. They were made as lessons to learn the fundamentals of patchwork, using scraps and offcuts.

One year, as I was designing the block-of-the-month programs for Material Obsession, I happened across a picture on Flickr of a wall full of doll quilts, and it made me recall the Amish doll quilts. What a perfect vehicle for a different kind of block-of-the-month! I started designing quilts for the program and my obsession with little quilts was born.

When I went out on my own it was a good place to begin. I started a doll quilt pattern program in Europe, wrote *Quilting from Little Things* (which is all about trying out a technique with a dolly quilt and moving up to a large quilt), and started playing with Amy! All of this brings us back to this book.

Amy and I began our online friendship about six years ago. In an initial exchange of emails we quickly discovered our mutual love of sarcasm, coffee, flavored beers, and gorgeous fabric. What more does a friendship need? There's something so intense about the online friendships we form these days. Having never met someone, we can feel like they are such an essential part of our everyday lives. I value Amy's friendship and talents and humor hugely, and my life would be so much the poorer without her. We are fortunate to be "real life" friends as well as digital ones, but for a long time our friendship was conducted though emails,

sarcastic Facebook messages and tweets, and boxes full of presents in the mail.

Dollies Online was such a fun thing for both of us. Amy was having a very difficult time, and so, in a different way, was I. Having walked away from a business that I had poured my heart and soul into, I had no idea what I was going to do next. Working with Amy helped me to see that I could do whatever I wanted and have such a good time doing it.

Each month we took turns sending a quilt in the mail—which was usually accompanied by a box of animal-shaped erasers, stickers, Lalaloopsy dolls, pens with sausage dogs on them, or chocolate—you get the picture. Not only were we having fun with the participants of the Dollies Online program, but also we each enjoyed so much the surprise of the quilt and the box (or the preparation of it) each month.

The quilts in this book were developed to be shared, swapped, and given as gifts, and that's what we hope you do with them. They are perfect for online swaps, quilt bees, gifts for quilty friends, or presents for special little people. If you aren't involved in any of those things, though, they make gorgeous cushions, table runners, or potholders. Amy and I have also developed a range of patterns based on making each quilt into a larger project (see page 124), so, if you want to "make them bigger," you can! This book is meant to be a collection of tiny ideas that are limited only by what you can think of to do with them. Have fun!

What a Star *by Sarah*

This is a quilt to showcase your scraps! Although the inset piecing is a little tricky, these stars sparkle and are well worth the effort. The blocks would make a wonderful large quilt, too.

Finished size

27 in. (68.5 cm) square

Note Seams are stitched with right sides together using a ¼ in. (6 mm) seam allowance unless otherwise stated.

Material requirements

• 2¼ in.- (5.7 cm-) wide strip of each of 16 different fabrics in a wide variety of colors and patterns for the stars

• ½ yd (50 cm) natural linen for background

• ¼ yd (25 cm) green fabric for binding

• 30 in. (76 cm) square of backing fabric

• 30 in. (76 cm) square of cotton batting (wadding)

• Cotton thread for piecing

• Template plastic (see page 106 for templates)

• Pencil for drawing on template plastic

• Scissors for cutting template plastic

• Kaleidoscope ruler (a triangular ruler used to cut the pieces required for 45-degree angles), optional

• Crewel embroidery no. 9 needles for hand quilting

• Dark brown perle 8 cotton for hand quilting

• Rotary cutter, mat, and ruler

• Sewing machine

• General sewing supplies

Cutting

From template plastic, cut:

• One Template A

• One Template B

• One Template C

From each of the 16 colored print fabrics, cut:

• One 2¼ in.- (5.7 cm-) wide strip for the star points— cross-cut each strip into eight 2¼ x 5 in. (5.7 x 12.7 cm) rectangles.

From the natural linen, cut:

• One 8½ in.- (21.6 cm-) wide strip—from this strip, cross-cut two 8½ in. (21.6 cm) squares and four 5 x 8½ in. (12.7 x 21.6 cm) rectangles.

• One 4½ in.- (11.4 cm-) wide strip—from this strip, cross-cut five 4½ in. (11.4 cm) squares. Trim the remainder of the strip to 4 in. (10.2 cm) wide and from it cut four Template B.

• One 3½ in.- (9 cm-) wide strip—from this strip, cut four Template C.

From the green binding fabric, cut:

• Three 3 in.- (7.5 cm-) wide strips

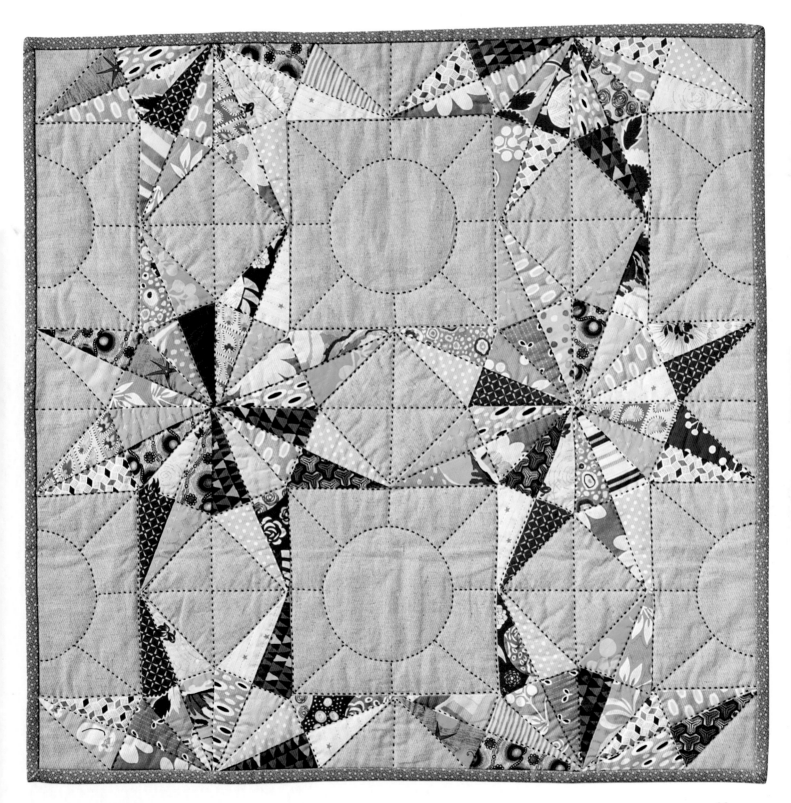

Star points

1 Sew the 2¼ x 5 in. (5.7 x 12.7 cm) colored print fabric rectangles into pairs along one long side, randomly mixing the colors. Press the seams to one side.

2 Sew two pairs together to form a four-patch unit (see Diagram 1). Press. Make 32.

3 Fold a four-patch unit in half along the short center seam. Place the ruler or Template A along the fold and cut through both layers along the 22½-degree angle (see Diagram 2). If using the kaleidoscope ruler, line up the 4¼ in. (10.8 cm) line on the ruler with the fold. Open out the unit to make a 45-degree diamond unit. Make 32.

Once you have cut the diamonds in step 3, do not press them again until after you have sewn the quilt together. Their edges are cut on the bias and they will stretch easily if ironed and make the quilt out of shape.

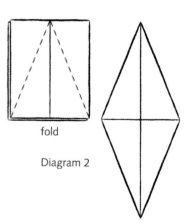

Diagram 1

fold

Diagram 2

Assembly

4 Sew four diamond units together to form a half-star unit (see Diagram 3), beginning and ending the stitching ¼ in. (6 mm) from the ends of the seams for ease of piecing. Make four.

5 Sew three diamond units together to form a three-point unit (see Diagram 4). Make four. Set the remaining four diamond units aside.

6 Arrange two half-star units and two three-point units as in Diagram 5, placing a 4½ in. (11.4 cm) linen square in each of the two squares created between the stars.

7 Begin sewing with the top piece in the row. Inset-piece the linen square into the "Y" seam between the points by beginning at the outside point and sewing along to ¼ in. (6 mm) from the fork of the "Y." Leave the needle down. Lift the presser foot and pivot the star and the fabric so that the next side of the square lies along the next arm of the star.

8 Make sure the fabrics are lying flat. You may need to lift the needle at this stage to do this. Put the needle back at the ¼ in. (6 mm) point of the seam and continue sewing out to the point of the star. Finger press the seam under the star.

9 Join the half-star unit to the linen square in the same way. Finger press the seam.

10 Repeat steps 7–9 with the other three pieces in the row. Sew the two sections together, forming a full star in the middle of the row. Make the second row in the same way as steps 6–10.

11 Using the same method, inset a 5 x 8½ in. (12.7 x 21.6 cm) linen rectangle into the outer edges of both rows (see Diagram 6). The rectangles are larger than required so the quilt can be trimmed square later.

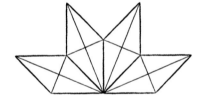

Diagram 3

Diagram 4

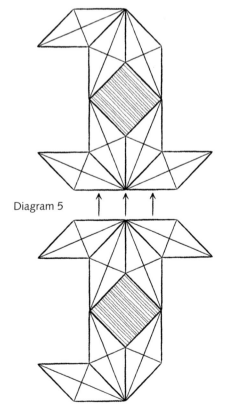

Diagram 5

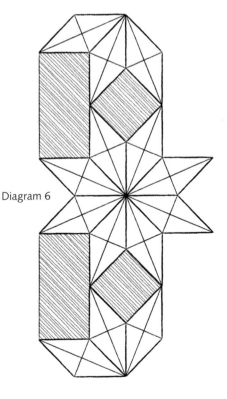

Diagram 6

12 Sew a Template C triangle into the center point of the outer star edges, and two Template B triangles to the corners of each row (see Diagram 7). The triangles are larger than required so the quilt can be trimmed square later.

13 Sew a diamond unit to each diagonal side of a Template C triangle (see Diagram 8). Make two.

14 Arrange the two rows next to each other with the points of the center stars touching, creating a square between the stars. Inset-piece a 4½ in. (11.4 cm) square into this space (see Diagram 9).

15 Inset-piece the two 8½ in. (21.6 cm) squares into the two large spaces between the stars. Finish the quilt top by inset-piecing the units from step 13 at the top and bottom of the quilt top (see Diagram 10).

16 Press the quilt.

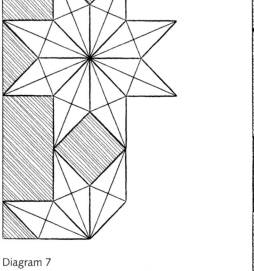

Diagram 7

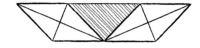

Diagram 8

Diagram 9

Diagram 10

Backing, quilting, and binding

17 Using the rotary cutter, mat, and ruler, square the quilt top, leaving ¼ in. (6 mm) beyond the outer star points.

18 Layer the backing, batting (wadding), and quilt top following the instructions on page 100.

19 Using dark brown perle 8 cotton thread, hand quilt around the linen pieces and the seams of the stars, following the instructions on page 102. Quilt a circle in the center of the large pieces and radiating lines to the star points.

20 Bind the quilt, following the instructions on page 104.

Candy is Dandy *by Amy*

My maternal grandfather was forever bringing us tasty treats, usually candy of some sort—chewy caramels, chocolate stars, nutty nougats, all wrapped in bright, shiny packaging. The cheerful narrow stripes in this quilt always remind me of the fruit-flavored hard candies I loved best.

Finished size

17 x 24½ in. (43 x 62 cm)

Note Seams are stitched with right sides together using a ¼ in. (6 mm) seam allowance unless otherwise stated.

Material requirements

• ¼ yd (25 cm) solid off-white fabric for background

• 6 x 10 in. (15 x 25.5 cm) each of solid brown, burgundy, fuchsia, green, orange, and purple fabric for candy wrappers

• ⅛ yd (15 cm) each of brown, green, orange, and purple striped fabrics for candy wrappers

• ¼ yd (25 cm) off-white print fabric for sashing and outer borders

• ¼ yd (25 cm) purple striped fabric for binding

• 20 x 27 in. (51 x 69 cm) backing fabric

• 20 x 27 in. (51 x 69 cm) batting (wadding)

• Cotton thread for piecing

• Rotary cutter, mat, and ruler

• Sewing machine

• General sewing supplies

Cutting

From the solid off-white background fabric, cut:

• Four 2¾ in. (7 cm) squares. Cross-cut these squares on both diagonals to yield 16 quarter-square triangles.

• Six 4¾ in. (12 cm) squares. Cross-cut these squares on both diagonals to yield 24 quarter-square triangles.

From the solid colored fabrics, cut:

• One 2¾ in. (7 cm) square of each of four colors. Cross-cut these squares on both diagonals to yield 16 quarter-square triangles.

• One 4¾ in. (12 cm) square of each of six colors. Cross-cut these squares on both diagonals to yield 24 quarter-square triangles.

From the striped fabrics, cut:

• One 4 in. (10 cm) square each of brown and green

• Two 4 in. (10 cm) squares each of orange and purple

• One 2 x 4 in. (5 x 10 cm) rectangle each of brown and orange

• Two 2 x 4 in. (5 x 10 cm) rectangles each of green and purple

From the off-white print fabric, cut:

• Four 2 x 21½ in. (5 x 54.5 cm) strips

From the purple striped binding fabric, cut:

• Three 2¼ in.- (6 cm-) wide strips

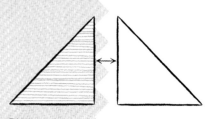

Diagram 1

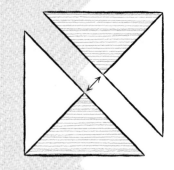

Diagram 2

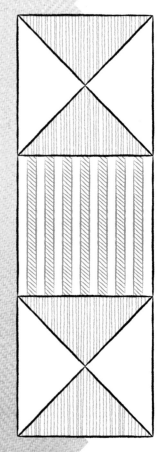

Diagram 3

Sewing

1 Sew the large solid-color triangles into pairs with the large off-white plain triangles (see Diagram 1). There should be two each of brown, burgundy, fuchsia, green, orange, and purple. Press the seams away from the off-white fabric.

2 Sew two matching pairs together to make a large quarter-square triangle block (see Diagram 2). Press the seams open. Make 12 blocks.

3 Sew a large quarter-square triangle block to the opposite ends of a 4 in. (10 cm) striped square to make a large candy wrapper block (see Diagram 3). Press the seams toward the striped square. Make six blocks.

4 In the same way as in step 1, sew the small solid-color triangles into pairs with the small off-white plain triangles. Press the seams away from the off-white fabric.

5 In the same way as in step 2, sew two matching pairs together to make a small quarter-square triangle block. Press the seams open. Make eight blocks.

6 Sew a small quarter-square triangle block to each end of a 2 x 4 in. (5 x 10 cm) striped rectangle (see Diagram 4). Press the seams toward the striped rectangles. Make four units in this way.

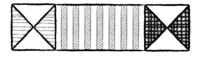

Diagram 4

Assembling the quilt top

7 Referring to the quilt layout, arrange the units and border strips so that the colors are distributed in a pleasing way.

8 Sew the large candy wrapper blocks into three pairs. Press the seams open.

9 Sew a 2 x 21½ in. (5 x 54.5 cm) off-white print sashing strip to each side of two large candy wrapper pairs. Press the seams toward the sashing strip.

10 Sew one of these units to each side of the remaining pair of large candy wrapper blocks. Press the seams toward the sashing.

11 Sew a small candy wrapper block to each end of a 2 x 4 in. (5 x 10 cm) striped rectangle (see Diagram 5). Press the seams toward the striped rectangle. Make two of these units.

12 Sew one of these units to each end of a 2 x 4 in. (5 x 10 cm) striped rectangle. Make two pieced strips in this way for the top and bottom borders.

13 Pin and then sew the top and bottom borders to the top and bottom edges of the quilt, aligning the small quarter-square triangle blocks with the off-white print sashing strips. Press the seams toward the borders.

Backing, quilting, and binding

14 Using the rotary cutter, mat, and ruler, square the quilt top if necessary.

15 Layer the backing, batting (wadding), and quilt top, following the instructions on page 100.

16 Quilt by machine or by hand as desired. I machine quilted all over the quilt in double teardrop shapes (see Diagram 13 on page 103).

17 Using the purple striped binding strips, bind the quilt, following the instructions on page 104.

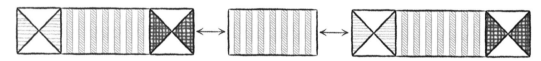

Diagram 5

Grandma's House *by Sarah*

Little Red is off through the woods to Grandma's house but doesn't know that the wolf got there first! Try your hand at improvisational piecing to make a fun, one-of-a-kind quilt.

Finished size

Approximately 21½ x 15½ in. (54.5 x 39.5 cm)—exact size will depend on sizes of pieces used

Note Seams are stitched with right sides together using a ¼ in. (6 mm) seam allowance unless otherwise stated.

Material requirements

• Scraps of at least four different green print fabrics for trees

• 25 in. (63.5 cm) dark blue print fabric for background

• Scraps of brown print fabric for tree trunks and chimney

• 4 in. (10 cm) white print fabric for house

• Fabric scraps for windows and door—the quilt pictured includes novelty prints to put a wolf and gnomes in the windows

• 8 in. (20.5 cm) square of brown print fabric for roof

• Scrap of green fabric for bottom left-hand corner—the quilt in the photograph has a unicorn in the forest.

• 6 in. (15 cm) red-and-white polka-dot fabric for cape and word "red"

• Scraps of white and brown fabrics for Little Red's face, dress, hands, and legs

• 4 in. (10 cm) light blue print fabric for sky above house and strips below and at sides

• 15 in. (38 cm) dark brown print fabric for binding, cut into 3 in.- (7.5 cm-) wide strips

• Approx 29 x 23 in. (73.5 x 58.5 cm) backing fabric

• Approx 29 x 23 in. (73.5 x 58.5 cm) cotton batting (wadding)

• Cotton thread for piecing

• Crewel embroidery no. 9 needles for hand quilting

• Aurifil Cotton 12 thread in green, orange, and red for hand quilting

• Rotary cutter, mat, and ruler

• Sewing machine

• General sewing supplies

Cutting

For the improvisational piecing technique, pieces of fabric are cut as needed, without using a ruler. This allows each quilt to be a one-off. Suggested cutting instructions for fabric pieces are given in the steps, but remember that these are guides only. Use a ruler to trim each unit straight.

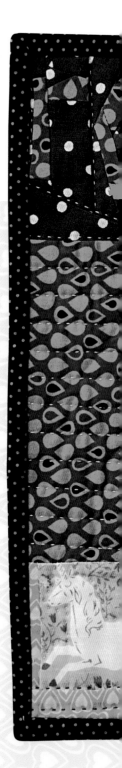

Trees

1 Cut a rough 3 in. (7.5 cm) square from each of three or four green fabrics, without using a ruler. To make longer, flatter tree pieces, cut rectangles instead of squares.

2 Sew a strip of dark blue print fabric to opposite sides of each square or rectangle (see Diagram 1). Make sure that the background fabric pieces will overlap at the point by at least ¼ in. (6 mm) or the tree will have a flat top (see Diagram 2). Trim away the excess green fabric behind the blue fabric, ¼ in. (6 mm) from the seam to reduce bulk. Make three to five of these units depending on the size of the fabric pieces. As long as the units are around the same size, they can fit together in height by adjusting the trunks of the trees.

3 Trim the top and bottom of each of the units from step 2 so they are straight (see Diagram 3). Sew them together in a vertical strip, one on top of another (see Diagram 4). Trim the sides of the tree strip straight (see Diagram 5).

4 Cut a 1¼ in.- (3 cm-) wide strip of brown print fabric for the trunk of the tree. Sew a dark blue print strip to the opposite sides of it. Trim the piece straight at the top and bottom and then sew it to the bottom of the largest tree. Press the piece and trim the edges square. Make two trees (or three or four if you want to change the quilt—that's the whole idea). It doesn't matter at this stage if they are different heights.

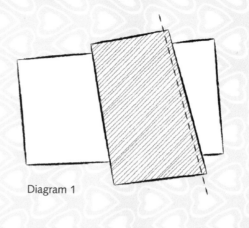

Diagram 1

Diagram 2

Diagram 3

Diagram 4

Diagram 5

House

5 From scraps (or novelty prints, as in photograph) cut two pieces approximately 3 x 2 in. (7.5 x 5 cm) for the house windows. Cut a strip of the white print house fabric and sew a piece of it in between the two windows, and two more pieces of it on either side of the windows. If you wish, add a strip of fabric beneath the windows to make the house a little taller.

6 Cut a piece of scrap fabric approximately 2 x 3½ in. (5 x 9 cm) for the door. Cut two pieces of white print house fabric roughly the same size as the door and sew them either side of the door.

7 Trim the edges of the windows and the door and then sew the pieces together. Press the house and trim the edges straight.

8 Sew a wide piece of dark blue print fabric to opposite sides of the house. Don't worry about trying to make the strip straight—it is supposed to be wonky. Trim the top and bottom of the house straight (see Diagram 6).

9 Cut a piece of brown print fabric for the roof, a little wider than the house. Make a pointed or flat-topped triangle with the brown print fabric and two pieces of dark blue fabric in much the same way as the tree triangles in step 2. Add a chimney, if you wish, by sewing it into the piece of background first, then attaching the background to the house roof at an angle.

10 Sew the roof to the top of the house and trim the whole piece straight (see Diagram 7).

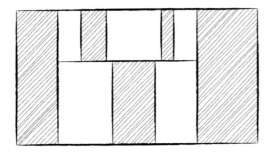

Diagram 6

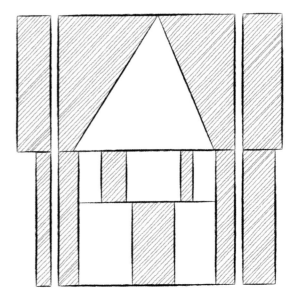

Diagram 7

The word "red"

11 Cut four or five 1½ in. (4 cm) strips from the dark blue print fabric and a rectangle approximately 2 x 1½ in. (5 x 4 cm) from the red-and-white polka-dot fabric. The size of the rectangle will determine the size of the space underneath the "r" and therefore the height of your letter (see Diagram 8).

12 Sew a strip of dark blue print fabric to each side of the top of the red-and-white polka-dot rectangle, making sure they overlap in the center (see Diagram 9) and trimming the excess from the first strip before attaching the next one. Press the seams toward the letter.

13 Sew a piece of red-and-white polka-dot fabric to the top right-hand side (see Diagram 10). Trim the excess, and then sew a piece to the left-hand side (see Diagram 11).

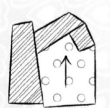

Diagram 8

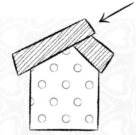

Diagram 9

Diagram 10

Diagram 11

14 Trim the left-hand side of the piece straight; press. Cut a piece of the dark blue print fabric long enough to be the straight edge of the "r." Add a piece of the polka-dot fabric to the top of this so that it is as long or longer than the curved part of the "r." Sew the piece to the left-hand side and press (see Diagram 12).

15 Add some extra strips of the polka-dot fabric around the "r" so that it "floats" in the background fabric. Leave at least ½ in. (1.2 cm) of polka-dot fabric on the right-hand side of the "r" so that the next letter can be attached.

16 Make the "e" and the "d" in the same manner.

17 When you have made the three letters, trim the right side of the "r," both sides of the "e," and the left side of the "d" straight line, ¼ in. (6 mm) from where you want the seam to be. Don't worry too much about the letters being the same height. If there isn't enough room for trimming, just sew an extra piece of dark blue print fabric to the top or bottom. Sew the letters together to spell "red" (see Diagram 13).

18 Trim a straight line around the edges of the word. The lines do not have to make a rectangle—they just have to be straight. Decide how you want the word to sit, and then sew extra fabric strips to the edges where needed and trim the word square. Sarah's "red" is approximately 4½ x 7½ in. (11.5 x 19 cm).

Diagram 12

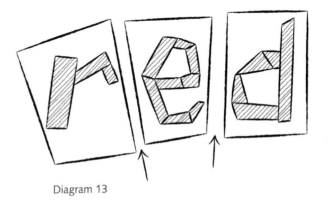

Diagram 13

If you are concerned about how to make the letters, try writing each one down before you begin to sew it. The letters are sewn the same way as you would draw them, for example with the "d" you would make the round part first and then add the straight side. Don't be afraid to add extra pieces of fabric to fill gaps—that's all part of the charm of this project. Your letters may look different to the ones in Sarah's quilt, but that's the fun of improvisational quilting!

Little Red

19 Little Red is constructed in the same way as all the other components of the quilt—by adding pieces of fabric until the motif takes shape. Cut a face about 1½ in. (4 cm) square from a white scrap, and sew red fabric around it to make a hood. Sew pieces of dark blue print fabric around the head and then trim the bottom edge of the head (along the neck) straight so it is ready to sew to the body.

20 Cut approximately 3½ x 1½ in. (9 x 4 cm) white print fabric for the dress. If you wish, add hands by inserting a ¾ in.- (2 cm-) wide strip of brown fabric in the center of the dress fabric, with a scrap of the white print in the middle of the brown strip.

21 Sew a piece of red-and-white polka-dot fabric on a diagonal to each side of the dress for the cape, and then a piece of dark blue print background fabric on each side of that. Trim the top edge of the dress straight, center the head on top of the dress, and sew the pieces together.

22 Cut two 1 x 2 in. (2.5 x 5 cm) pieces of dark brown fabric for legs. Sew a small piece of dark blue print fabric between them. Sew a strip of the dark blue print to the outside of the legs, trim the top straight, and then sew them to Little Red's body. Ensure there is enough dark blue print fabric all around to square the unit, adding more strips if necessary, and then trim the edges straight.

Assembly

23 Referring to the quilt photograph, arrange the pieces of the quilt. You may decide to put your house on the other side or have more space above the trees—it's your quilt so anything goes. Cut strips of light blue print fabric for the sky and a strip to go along the bottom of the quilt.

24 Sew pieces of dark blue print fabric to fill the gaps between shapes, and add extra pieces of the appropriate fabric to make the trees higher or to make Little Red match the height of the house. The pieces in the quilt will join in straight lines as long as you find the straight lines that suit your design (see Diagram 14).

25 Sew all the units together and press.

Backing, quilting, and binding

26 Using the rotary cutter, mat, and ruler, square the quilt top, if necessary.

27 Layer the backing, batting (wadding) and quilt top, following the instructions on page 100.

28 Using Aurifil Cotton 12 thread in green, hand quilt lines across the background, spacing them ½ in. (1.2 cm) apart and following the instructions on page 102. Using green, orange, or red thread, quilt around the outlines of the trees and the house.

29 Bind the quilt, following the instructions on page 104.

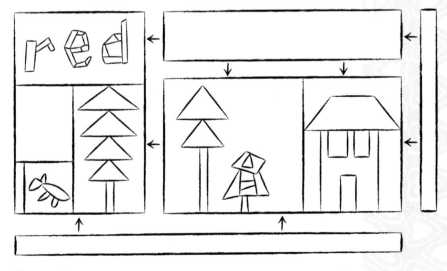

Diagram 14

Baskets

Polka-dot Baskets *by Amy*

Whenever I see anything with red-and-white polka-dots, I immediately think of Sarah, so I made this perky polka-dot basket quilt for her birthday. In another small ode to her, I added contrast perle cotton hand quilting. The baskets are fused and feature raw-edge stitching.

Finished size

21½ x 17 in. (54.5 x 43 cm)

Note Seams are stitched with right sides together using a ¼ in. (6 mm) seam allowance unless otherwise stated.

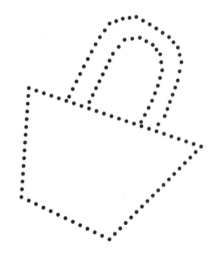

Material requirements

• 6½ x 8½ in. (16.5 x 21.5 cm) each of six cream print fabrics for basket backgrounds

• 2½ in. (6.2 cm) cream print fabric for border

• Six 8½ in. (21.5 cm) squares of red-and-white polka-dot fabrics for basket bases and sashings

• 8½ in. (21.5 cm) square of solid black fabric for basket handles

• ¼ yd (25 cm) solid cream fabric for filler blocks, sashings, and border

• 5 in. (13 cm) red-and-white polka-dot fabric for binding

• 18 x 24 in. (45.5 x 61 cm) backing fabric

• 18 x 24 in. (45.5 x 61 cm) cotton batting (wadding)

• White, cream, and black perle 8 cotton for embroidery and quilting

• Crewel embroidery no. 9 needles for hand quilting

• Fusible web

• Black cotton thread for machine appliqué stitching

• Cotton thread for piecing

• Rotary cutter, mat, and ruler

• Sewing machine

• General sewing supplies

Cutting

The "(for B1)," "(for B2)," etc, shown below, indicates a piece is used in Basket 1, Basket 2, and so on, as shown in the block layout.

From the cream print fabrics, cut:

- Two 6½ in. (16.5 cm) squares (for B1, B5)

- Three 4½ in. (11.5 cm) squares (for B2, B3, B6)

- One 4½ x 8½ in. (11.5 x 21.5 cm) rectangle (for B4)

- One 2½ x 17½ in. (6.2 x 44.2 cm) strip (for border)

From the red-and-white polka-dot fabrics, cut:

- Two 6½ in. (16.5 cm) squares (for B1, B5)

- Three 4½ in. (11.5 cm) squares (for B2, B3, B6)

- One 4½ x 8½ in. (11.5 x 21.5 cm) rectangle (for B4)

- One 1 x 8 in. (2.5 x 20.5 cm) rectangle (for B1)

- One 1½ x 6½ in. (3.9 x 16.5 cm) rectangle (for B1)

- One 2 x 6 in. (4.7 x 15 cm) rectangle (for B3)

- One 1 x 8½ in. (2.5 x 21.5 cm) rectangle (for B4)

- One 1¾ x 4½ in. (4.5 x 11.5 cm) rectangle (for B6)

- One 1¼ x 6½ in. (3 x 16.5 cm) rectangle (for B6)

- One 2½ x 4½ in. (6.2 x 11.5 cm) rectangle (for border)

From the solid cream fabric, cut:

- One 2 x 7½ in. (5.2 x 19.2 cm) rectangle (for B1)

- One 3 x 6½ in. (7.5 x 16.5 cm) rectangle (for B2)

- One 1½ x 6½ in. (3.9 x 16.5 cm) rectangle (for B2)

- One 2½ x 4½ in. (6.2 x 11.5 cm) rectangle (for B2)

- One 2 x 4½ in. (4.7 x 11.5 cm) rectangle (for B3)

- One 1½ x 8½ in. (3.4 x 21.5 cm) rectangle (for B4)

- One 1¾ x 6½ in. (4.2 x 16.5 cm) rectangle (for B5)

- One 1¼ x 4½ in. (2.9 x 11.5 cm) rectangle (for B6)

- One 1 x 6½ in. (2.4 x 16.5 cm) rectangle (for B6)

- One 1½ x 6½ in. (3.7 x 16.5 cm) rectangle (for B6)

- Two 1½ x 14 in. (3.7 x 35.5 cm) strips (for border)

- One 1½ x 21½ in. (3.7 x 54.5 cm) strip (for border)

From the binding fabric, cut:

Two 2¼ in.- (6 cm-) wide strips

Appliqué

1 Trace the six basket bases on pages 108–109 onto the paper side of fusible web, spacing them at least ½ in. (1.2 cm) apart. Cut out the shapes leaving approximately ¼ in. (6 mm) beyond the drawn lines. Following the manufacturer's directions, fuse the fusible web to the wrong side of the red-and-white polka-dot fabrics. Cut the basket bases out along the drawn lines.

2 Trace the basket handles onto the paper side of the fusible web, grouping them together. Add ¼ in. (6 mm) to the ends of the handles so they can be tucked under the basket bases later. Fuse the fusible web to the wrong side of the black fabric. Cut the basket handles out on the drawn lines.

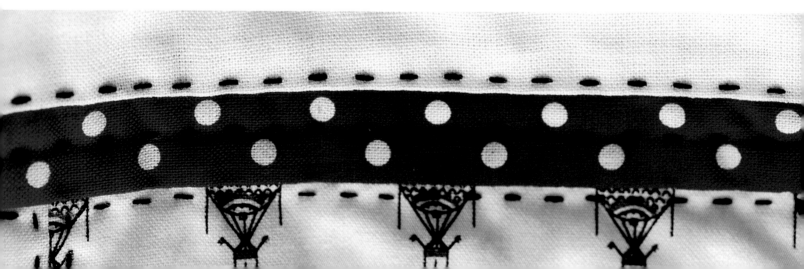

3 Position Basket 1 and its handle on a 6½ in. (16.5 cm) square of cream print fabric, tucking the ends of the handle under the basket base. Fuse the basket and handle in place. In the same way, fuse the remaining basket bases and handles in place on the correct cream print fabric piece (see block layout).

4 Using black thread in the sewing machine, straight stitch or free-motion stitch on the appliqué shapes approximately ⅛ in. (3 mm) from the raw edges of the baskets and handles. If you would like a more defined look, stitch over the first row of stitching.

If preferred, use a buttonhole stitch or narrow zigzag stitch instead. Alternatively, the basket bases and handles can be appliquéd using the needle-turn technique (see page 96).

Embroidery

5 Trace the "Baskets" text from the photograph (or write your choice of words on the quilt, or print off in your chosen font, then trace) onto a 3 x 6½ in. (7 x 16.5 cm) solid cream rectangle. Using black perle thread, backstitch (see Honeycomb Diagram 8, page 82) along the drawn line.

Sewing

6 Arrange all the pieces for the blocks as shown on the block layout below, which shows the sewing order for each block. For example, a 1½ x 6½ in. (3.9 x 16.5 cm) red-and-white polka-dot rectangle is sewn to the Basket 1 block first, followed by a 2 x 7½ in. (5.2 x 19.2 cm) solid cream rectangle, and then a 1 x 8 in. (2.5 x 20.5 cm) red-and-white polka-dot rectangle. Sew the six basket units, pressing the seams after each piece is added.

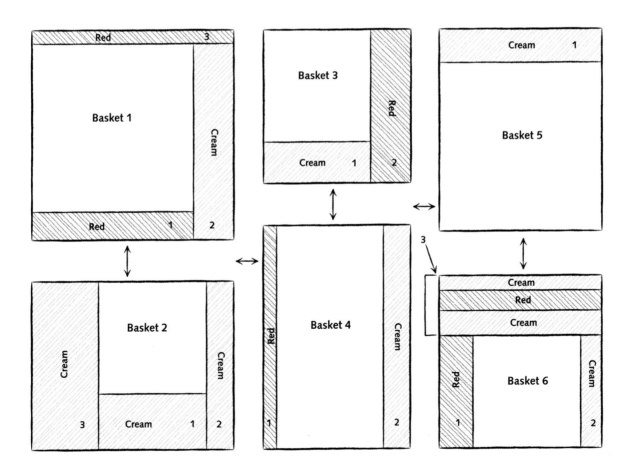

7 Once the units are complete, sew them together in this order, pressing each seam before adding the next block: Sew Basket 1 to Basket 2; sew Basket 3 to Basket 4; sew Basket 5 to Basket 6.

8 Now sew those units together in this order, pressing each seam before adding the next unit: Sew Basket 1/2 to Basket 3/4 and then sew Basket 5/6 to Basket 3/4.

Borders

9 Fold the two 1½ x 14 in. (3.7 x 35.5 cm) solid cream border strips in half, end to end, and mark the centers with pins. Mark the side edges of the quilt top in the same way. Matching the pins and with right sides together, pin a border strip to each side edge of the quilt top. Sew the borders to the quilt top. Press the seams toward the borders.

10 In the same way, pin and then sew one 1½ x 21½ in. (3.7 x 54.5 cm) solid cream border strip to the top edge of the quilt top. Press the seam toward the border.

11 Sew a 2½ x 4½ in. (6.5 x 11.5 cm) red-and-white polka-dot rectangle to the end of a 2½ x 17½ in. (6.2 x 44.2 cm) cream print strip, and press the seam. Pin and then sew the strip to the bottom edge of the quilt top; press the seam.

Backing, quilting, and binding

12 Using the rotary cutter, mat, and ruler, square the quilt top if necessary.

13 Layer the backing, batting (wadding), and quilt top, following the instructions on page 100.

14 Using white, cream, or black perle cotton thread, hand quilt around each block following the instructions on page 102.

15 Bind the quilt, following the instructions on page 104.

16 Using black perle cotton thread, hand quilt around the borders, just inside the binding.

Not Quite Hawaiian *by Sarah*

Not Quite Hawaiian—because it is Hawaiian appliqué, but not quite! Perhaps this design is a little more Scandinavian in flavor? Regardless, the technique is there, with just a hint of tropical delights. This is fairly complex needle-turn appliqué, so go slowly and be kind on yourself.

Finished size

18 in. (45.5 cm) square

Material requirements

- 20 in. (51 cm) blue-and-white print fabric for background
- 20 in. (51 cm) dark blue print fabric for appliqué
- 9 in. (23 cm) dark blue print fabric for binding
- 22 in. (56 cm) square of backing fabric
- 22 in. (56 cm) square of cotton batting (wadding)
- Cotton thread for appliqué, to match dark blue print fabric
- Appliqué needles
- 9 in. (23 cm) square of template plastic
- Pencil for tracing on template plastic
- Scissors for cutting template plastic
- Silver gel pen
- Sharp, small scissors for cutting appliqué
- 18 in. (45.5 cm) square of fusible web (if using iron-on method)
- Stranded embroidery floss and crewel needle, or cotton thread for machine appliqué (if using iron-on method)
- Crewel embroidery needles no. 9 for hand quilting
- Dark blue perle 8 cotton for hand quilting
- Rotary cutter, mat, and ruler
- Sewing machine
- General sewing supplies

Cutting

From the template plastic:

- One Motif Template (quarter of motif) (see page 107 for template)

From the blue-and-white print fabric, cut:

- One 20 in. (51 cm) square

From the dark blue print fabric, cut:

- One 18 in. (45.5 cm) square

From the dark blue print binding fabric, cut:

- Two 3 in.- (7.5 cm-) wide strips

If you have tried Sarah's method of needle-turn appliqué previously, read on and enjoy making your quilt. If you have not, please read the needle-turn appliqué instructions on page 96 carefully before cutting or sewing anything. Even if you are familiar with needle-turn appliqué, read the project instructions closely, as there are a few things you need to know about Hawaiian appliqué that are different, including the reverse appliqué component. And if you prefer not to use the needle-turn method, instructions are also included for the alternative, iron-on method—see the box opposite.

Needle-turn appliqué

1 Fold the background square into quarters and finger-press creases to find the center. The background square is larger than the finished quilt because it allows room to appliqué and for the outside edges of the background fabric to fray. The quilt top will be trimmed after the appliqué is complete.

2 Press the appliqué fabric into quarters. Place the template along one crease on the right side of the fabric and, using a silver gel pen, carefully trace one quarter of the shape. Repeat in all four quarters of the fabric.

3 Cut the outside edge of the appliqué shape back to a scant ¼ in. (6 mm) along the edge. Finger-press along the silver gel line around the piece you have cut out. Do not clip down into the curves or "V" shapes and do not cut out the center of the shape.

4 Press the background fabric into quarters. Center the appliqué piece on the background. This project is not suited to liquid appliqué glue because of the fine lines of the appliqué shape, so use a contrasting thread to baste (tack) along the inside of all the appliqué to anchor it to the background (see Diagram 1).

5 Thread your appliqué needle with thread to match the appliqué fabric. Following the instructions on page 96, appliqué around the outside of the shape.

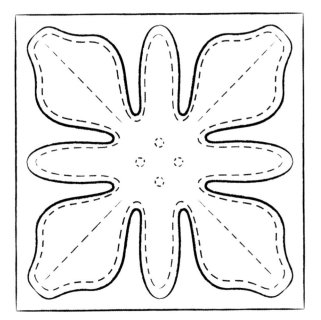

Diagram 1

Iron-on appliqué (alternative method)

If you prefer not to use the needle-turn appliqué method, replace steps 2–7 with this alternative method. Use the template to trace the whole motif onto the paper side of fusible web. Cut out the shape roughly outside, not on, the drawn line, and fuse the web to the back of the appliqué fabric following the manufacturer's instructions. Cut the fabric shape out on the drawn lines, including the holes, and position it on the background fabric, using the creases as a guide. Fuse in place. Either use two strands of embroidery floss and a crewel needle to blanket stitch or buttonhole stitch (see Diagram 5, page 81) along all the raw edges, or machine appliqué in place.

6 Using your thumb and forefinger, pinch the background fabric in the "hole" shapes away from the appliqué fabric. While they are held apart, use very sharp, small scissors to clip a small hole in the part of the appliqué fabric you are cutting away. Carefully clip away the appliqué fabric leaving a scant ¼ in. (6 mm) seam allowance (see Diagram 2), and finger-press around the gel line.

7 Clip any inside curves within the seam allowance, then sweep the fabric underneath the main appliqué shape and stitch in place. That's all there is to it! You just learned basic reverse appliqué.

Backing, quilting, and binding

8 Using the rotary cutter, mat, and ruler, trim the quilt top 1 in. (2.5 cm) outside the appliqué shape.

9 Layer the backing, batting (wadding), and quilt top, following the instructions on page 100.

10 Using dark blue perle cotton, hand quilt around the shapes following the instructions on page 102.

11 Bind the quilt, following the instructions on page 104.

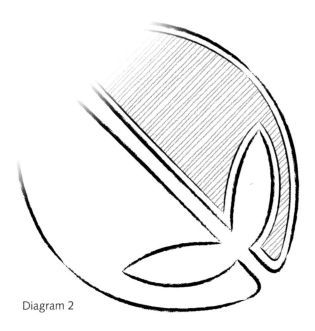

Diagram 2

Pretty Little Half Hex *by Amy*

I can't resist sweet little hexagons! This quilt cuts the hexagon in half and allows you to embrace machine piecing. Don't let a "Y" seam intimidate you —it really is very manageable at the machine. Pretty Little Half Hex mixes low-volume and saturated favorite prints in a limited color palette of pink, green, gold, and brown. Four focus hexagons lend cohesion to the layout.

Finished size

12¼ x 17½ in. (31.1 x 44.5 cm)

Note Seams are stitched with right sides together using a ¼ in. (6 mm) seam allowance unless otherwise stated.

Material requirements

• ½ yd (45 cm) assorted print fabrics for the hexagons— minimum size 1½ x 3¼ in. (4 x 8.5 cm)

• One fat quarter of backing fabric

• 18 x 21 in. (45.5 x 53.5 cm) batting (wadding)

• ¼ yd (25 cm) brown print for binding

• 2 x 4 in. (5 x 10 cm) template plastic (see page 114 for template)

• Pencil for tracing on template plastic

• Scissors for cutting template plastic

• Cotton thread for piecing

• Rotary cutter, mat, and ruler

• Sewing machine

• General sewing supplies

When choosing fabrics, select a limited color palette but use lots of different prints. Fat quarters are great for this project because a single 1½ x 21 in. (4 x 53 cm) strip from a fat quarter yields five half hexagons. If using fat-quarter strips, 24 are required.

Cutting

From the template plastic, cut:

• One Half Hexagon Template

From the assorted strips, cut:

• 119 half hexagons

From the binding fabric, cut:

• Two 2¼ in.- (6 cm-) wide strips

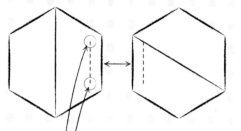

Diagram 1

Stitch together starting ¼ in. (6 mm) from raw edges.

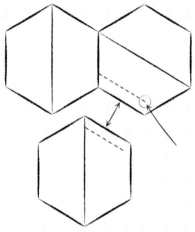

Diagram 2

Stitch together starting ¼ in. (6 mm) from raw edges.

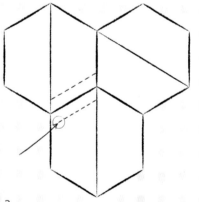

Diagram 3

Stitch together starting ¼ in. (6 mm) from raw edges.

Sewing

1 Sew two matching half hexagons together along the long seam line to make a hexagon. Press the seams open. Make four, which will be the centers of the four focus hexagons. Trim the "ears" (the "dog-ear" triangles at the beginning and end of each seam) from the hexagons.

2 Sew 52 pairs of unmatching half hexagons along the long center seam line to make 52 hexagons. Press the seams open. Trim off the "ears." Reserve the remaining seven half hexagons.

3 Only a focus hexagon has half hexagons in two fabrics alternating around a center hexagon. (The other half hexagons attached to these half hexagons vary.) Refer to the quilt layout and the quilt photograph, and for each focus hexagon select three hexagons in which the half hexagons are in one fabric and three more hexagons that have half hexagons in a second fabric, to alternate around the center. Do this for all four focus hexagons.

When piecing the remainder of the quilt after step 2, do not press the seams until the entire quilt has been sewn together. Then carefully press all seams open, making sure there are no lumpy seam allowances folded under themselves. Use a stiletto or the end of a seam ripper to ensure seam allowances are neatly pressed.

4 With right sides together, sew one of the hexagons from step 3 to a center hexagon along the short flat seam, starting and stopping ¼ in. (6 mm) from the raw edges (see Diagram 1).

5 Sew a neighboring hexagon to the center hexagon in the "Y" between the hexagons. Begin ¼ in. (6 mm) from the raw edge and sew along to ¼ in. (6 mm) from the fork of the "Y" (see Diagram 2). Leave the needle down.

6 Lift the presser foot and pivot the pieces so that the next side of the hexagon is correctly placed and the fabrics are lying flat. You may need to lift the needle at this stage to do this. Put the needle back at the ¼ in. (6 mm) point of the seam and continue sewing out to ¼ in. (6 mm) from the raw edge (see Diagram 3).

7 Repeat steps 4, 5, and 6 with the remaining four hexagons to form a focus hexagon. Make four focus hexagons.

Assembly

8 Referring to the quilt layout, arrange all the hexagons and remaining half hexagons to create a pleasing pattern. The center seams of the hexagons can be oriented in any direction.

9 Sew the shapes together. It is easiest to sew flat seams first and then sew short angled seams with the "Y" seam method described in step 5.

10 Press all the seams open.

Backing, quilting, and binding

11 Using the rotary cutter, mat, and ruler, trim the side points as shown in the quilt layout.

12 Layer the backing, batting (wadding), and quilt top, following the instructions on page 100.

13 Quilt by machine or by hand as desired. The quilt pictured has been machine quilted all over in double teardrop shapes (see Diagram 13, page 103).

14 Bind the quilt, following the instructions on page 104.

After top is pieced together, trim off side points

Quilt layout

My Heart *by Sarah*

This quilt would make a lovely gift for someone close to your heart. The little blocks are quick to appliqué and it makes a lovely carry-around project. If you fussy-cut the hearts, you can display your favorite fabrics through the little windows.

Finished size

18½ in. (47 cm) square

Note Seams are stitched with right sides together using a ¼ in. (6 mm) seam allowance unless otherwise stated.

Material requirements

• 5 in. (13 cm) solid brown fabric for heart blocks

• Eight pieces brightly colored scrap fabric for heart blocks, no smaller than 4½ in. (11.5 cm) square

• 16 pieces of brightly colored scrap fabric for windmill blocks, no smaller than 4 x 6 in. (10 x 15 cm)

• 3 in. (7.5 cm) yellow-on-white polka-dot fabric for border

• 6 in. (15 cm) brown print fabric for binding

• 24 in. (61 cm) square of backing fabric

• 24 in. (61 cm) square of cotton wadding (batting)

• 4 x 7 in. (10 x 18 cm) template plastic (see page 114 for templates)

• Pencil for tracing on template plastic

• Scissors for cutting template plastic

• Neutral cotton thread for piecing

• Silver gel pen

• Appliqué glue

• Small, sharp scissors for cutting reverse appliqué

• Appliqué needles

• Brown cotton thread for appliqué

• Crewel embroidery no. 9 needles for hand quilting

• Variegated orange/blue perle 8 cotton for hand quilting

• Rotary cutter, mat, and ruler

• Sewing machine

• General sewing supplies

Cutting

From the template plastic, cut:

• One Template A (windmill)

• One Template B (heart)

From the solid brown background fabric, cut:

• Eight 4½ in. (11.5 cm) squares

From each of the eight brightly colored scrap fabrics for the hearts, cut:

• One 4½ in. (11.5 cm) square—fussy-cut them (position each to take into account the fabric pattern) if you wish.

From each of the 16 brightly colored scrap fabrics for the windmills, cut:

• Four Template A—make sure that you cut all the pieces with the template right side up.

From the yellow-on-white polka-dot fabric, cut:

• Two 1½ in.- (4 cm-) wide strips

From the brown print fabric for the binding, cut:

• Two 3 in.- (7.5 cm-) wide strips

Windmill blocks

1 Separate the brightly colored Template A pieces into pairs of contrasting pieces. Place two with right sides together along the diagonal edge, offsetting them ¼ in. (6 mm) from each end (see Diagram 1). Sew the pieces together. Make four units. Press each seam toward the darker fabric.

2 Arrange the four units to form a windmill block (see Diagram 2). Sew two of these units into a pair and then repeat with the other two. Sew the two pairs together to form a square block, with the small end of each windmill piece always toward the center of the block. Press. The windmills should look more like kisses and not be symmetrical, so you will see that this block is now larger than 4½ in. (11.5 cm).

3 Using the ruler on top of the block, line up the 2¼ in. (5.75 cm) mark on the ruler with the center seam of the block. Using this as a guide, trim the block to 4½ in. (11.5 cm) square, and then press. Make eight windmill blocks in this way.

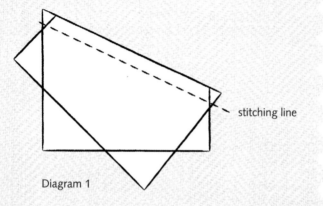

stitching line

Diagram 1

Diagram 2

Heart blocks

4 Fold a 4½ in. (11.5 cm) brown square into quarters and finger press the creases. Position Template B over the middle of the square on the right side of the fabric using the creases as a guide to finding the center.

5 Trace around Template B using a silver gel pen.

6 Put a few drops of appliqué glue on the wrong side of the brown square, toward the edge. Do not put the appliqué glue under the drawn heart shape, or closer than ¼ in. (6 mm) from the outer edge of the heart shape.

7 Place a 4½ in. (11.5 cm) brightly colored scrap fabric square right side up under the brown square. Glue the two pieces together. Wait a few moments for the glue to dry.

8 With your fingers, pinch the brown fabric inside the drawn heart away from the layer of brightly colored scrap fabric. Using small, sharp scissors cut the brown fabric away from the scrap fabric, ¼ in. (6 mm) inside the drawn heart outline.

9 On the brown fabric, carefully clip the curves and clip into the point at the "V" of the heart, clipping only within the ¼ in. (6 mm) seam allowance.

10 Finger press the clipped seam allowance around the drawn line of the heart, pressing the fabric underneath the brown square.

11 Thread an appliqué needle with brown cotton thread and begin sewing around the heart shape, taking small stitches and grabbing just the very edge of the fabric. Push the fabric underneath the brown square as you sew—don't try to pin or hold it all under at once, just work on the section you are sewing.

12 When you have sewn around the heart, reverse appliquéing the brown fabric to the scrap fabric, press the block.

13 Turn over the block and pull the glued pieces away from each other. Carefully cut the brightly colored scrap fabric away from the back of the brown square, ¼ in. (6 mm) outside the appliquéd heart. Make eight heart blocks in this way.

Assembly

14 Join four blocks together into a row, alternating the windmills and heart blocks. Refer to the photo of the quilt on page 45 for placement. Press. Repeat with the other blocks to make four rows. Join the four rows together to form the center of the quilt top, and press again.

Border

15 Measure the quilt top from one side edge to the other through the center to get the true measurement. It should measure 16½ in. (41.4 cm). Cut one strip to this measurement from each of the two polka-dot strips.

16 Fold each of these strips in half and mark the centers with pins. Mark the centers of the top and bottom edges of the quilt top in the same way. Matching the pins and with right sides together, pin a border strip to the top edge and another to the bottom edge. Sew the borders to the quilt top (see page 100). Press the seams.

17 Measure the quilt top from top to bottom through the center, it should be 18½ in. (47 cm). Cut the remaining polka-dot strips to this length. Pin and then sew the borders to the side edges of the quilt top. Press the seams.

Backing, quilting, and binding

18 Using the rotary cutter, mat, and ruler, square the quilt top if necessary.

19 Layer the backing, batting (wadding), and quilt top, following the instructions on page 100.

20 Using variegated blue and orange perle 8 cotton thread, hand quilt around the shapes following the instructions on page 102.

21 Bind the quilt, following the instructions on page 104.

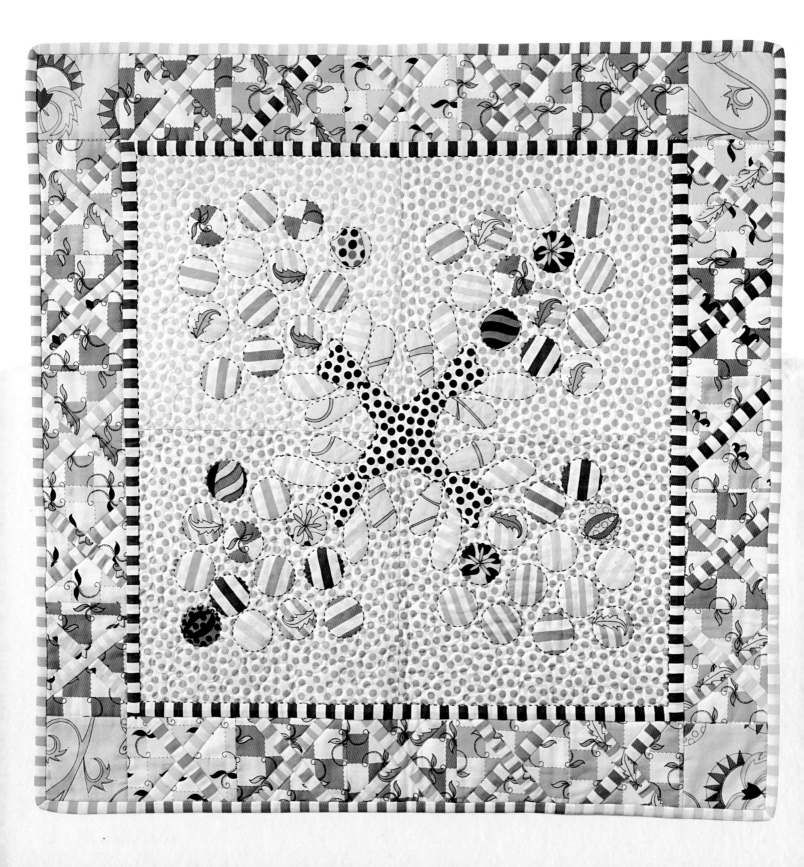

Apple Orchard *by Amy*

Apple Orchard was inspired by an antique quilt featuring appliqué blocks depicting apple trees. The folk art feel and whimsy of the antique quilt were hard to ignore. The apples line up side by side on my quilt, surrounding the tree trunks across the center. The appliqué on Apple Orchard was done with a hand-look machine-appliqué technique but it could easily be stitched by a needle-turn method, if preferred.

Finished size

26 in. (66.6 cm) square

Note Seams are stitched with right sides together using a ¼ in. (6 mm) seam allowance unless otherwise stated.

Material requirements

• 11 in. (28 cm) square each of four polka-dot fabrics for center background

• ¾ yd (70 cm) assorted striped fabrics for apples, leaves, inner border, and fence post blocks

• ½ yd (50 cm) assorted checked print fabrics for apples and fence post blocks

• ⅛ yd (15 cm) gray print fabric for cornerstones

• ¼ yd (25 cm) striped fabric for binding

• 7½ in. (19 cm) square of contrasting polka-dot fabric for tree base and trunks

• ⅛ yd (15 cm) each of two green print fabrics for leaves

• ⅞ yd (80 cm) backing fabric

• 30 in. (76 cm) square piece of batting (wadding)

• Cotton thread for piecing and machine quilting

• Clear monofilament thread for appliqué

• Rotary cutter, mat, and ruler

• 9 x 12 in. (23 x 30.5 cm) sheet of heat-resistant template plastic (see pages 110–111 for templates)

• Mechanical pencil for tracing on template plastic (do not use a permanent marker)

• Scissors for cutting template plastic

• Emery board

• Chalk pencil

• Spray starch or sizing and small plastic bowl

• Small, stiff stenciling brush or orange stick

• Small iron

• Basting glue or small appliqué pins

• Sewing machine with open-toe embroidery foot or zigzag foot

• Size 8/60 Microtex sewing machine needles

• General sewing supplies

Cutting

From the heat-resistant template plastic, cut:

• One Template A (tree base)

• One each Templates B–E (tree trunks)

• One each Templates F–M (leaves)

• One Template N (apple)

After cutting, erase any pencil marks on the plastic templates to prevent any marks transferring to the fabric when they become wet with starch and are pressed. (This is why a mechanical pencil rather than a permanent marker is used to trace the shapes onto the plastic.) Use an emery board to smooth any rough edges, because fabrics will conform exactly to the plastic shapes and imperfections could be transferred to the fabric.

From the assorted striped fabrics, cut:

• Two matching 1 x 19½ in. (2.5 x 49.6 cm) strips and two matching 1 x 20½ in. (2.5 x 52.2 cm) strips for the inner border

• Forty 1 x 8 in. (2.5 x 20.5 cm) strips for the fence post blocks

From the assorted checked print fabrics, cut:

• Twenty 4½ x 5½ in. (11.5 x 14 cm) rectangles

From the gray print fabric, cut:

• Four 3½ in. (9 cm) squares

From the striped binding fabric, cut:

• Three 2¼ in.- (6 cm-) wide strips

Cutting the appliqué shapes

To trace the appliqué shapes, place the template on the wrong side of the relevant fabric and draw around it with a chalk pencil. Cut out the fabric pieces, allowing a ¼ in. (6 mm) seam allowance outside the drawn line.

From the contrasting polka-dot fabric, cut:

• One Template A

• One each Templates B–E

From each of the two green print fabrics, cut:

• Two each Templates F–M (16 leaves in total)

From the various prints, cut:

• 52 Template N

Sewing

1 Sew the four 11 in. (28 cm) polka-dot fabric squares together to make a four-patch for the background. It should measure 21½ in. (54.8 cm).

Appliqué

2 Put some starch or sizing into a small plastic bowl and wait for the foam to turn to liquid, if necessary. For the tree base, trunks, and leaves, paint the seam allowances of a piece with starch on the wrong side of the fabric, doing short sections at a time rather than the whole shape at once. Place the plastic template on the wrong side of the fabric piece and use a small, stiff stencil brush or an orange stick to bring the seam allowances over the template edges.

3 Set a small iron to a medium temperature, so it is warm enough to dry the wet seams without buckling the template plastic. Press the appliqué seam allowances until just dry. Carefully remove the plastic template and press again.

If you don't have a small iron, you can use a regular-size one for pressing the appliqué seam allowances if you take great care. However, a small one is recommended because of the risk of burning your fingers.

4 For each apple circle, hand sew a running stitch (not a large basting stitch) inside the seam allowance around the circle. Knot the end of the thread, leaving a long tail. Place the plastic template on the wrong side of the fabric along the traced lines, and gather the stitching with the template inside. Holding the end of the thread, paint the seam allowance with starch and press to dry, as above. Loosen a few stitches and carefully remove the circle template, then press the circle again. Trim the long thread, leaving the running stitches in place.

5 Referring to the quilt layout, arrange the appliqué pieces on the pieced background square. Baste in place with basting glue or small appliqué pins.

6 To get a hand-look appliqué by machine, use a very small blind stitch and clear monofilament thread on both the top of the sewing machine and the bobbin. The best stitch choice is one that takes a few straight stitches and then one small step into the fabric, but a narrow buttonhole stitch will also work. Stitch each piece in place, lining up the shape so that the straight stitches will be in the background fabric just on the outside of the shape but every few stitches a

little "V" will bite into the appliqué shape. Finish by sewing over the first ¼ in. (6 mm) of stitching; no knotting or backstitching is necessary since the stitching is so fine.

7 When the appliqué is complete, lay it face down on a small towel and press from the wrong side.

8 Trim the quilt top to 19½ in. (49.6 cm) square, ensuring that the appliqué is still centered on the background.

Inner border

9 Fold the 1 x 19½ in. (2.5 x 49.6 cm) striped inner border strips in half and mark the centers with pins. Mark the top and bottom of the quilt top in the same way. Matching the pins and with right sides together, pin a strip to the top and bottom of the quilt top. Sew the borders to the quilt top (see page 100). Press the seams toward the center.

10 In the same way, pin and then sew the two 1 x 20½ in. (2.5 x 52.2 cm) inner border strips to the sides of the quilt top. Press the seams toward the center.

Fence post blocks

11 Cross-cut a 4½ x 5½ in. (11.5 x 14 cm) checked rectangle diagonally approximately ½ in. (1.2 cm) from the corners (see Diagram 1).

12 With right sides together, sew a 1 x 8 in. (2.5 x 20.5 cm) striped strip to one side of the diagonal cut. Press the seam toward the strip.

13 Center the other half of the rectangle along the other long edge of the strip, right sides together, and stitch (see Diagram 2). Press the seam toward the strip.

14 Cross-cut the rectangle diagonally approximately ½ in. (1.2 cm) from the other corners (see Diagram 3).

15 Take a 1 x 8 in. (2.5 x 20.5 cm) striped strip that contrasts with the one in steps 11–13, and sew it to one side of the diagonal cut. Press the seam toward the strip.

16 Center the other half of the rectangle along the strip and sew together (see Diagram 4). Press the seam toward the strip.

17 Trim the block to 3½ x 4½ in. (9 x 11.4 cm). Make 20 fence post blocks in this way.

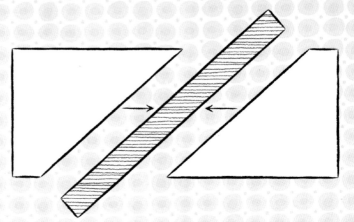

Diagram 2

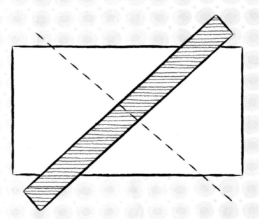

Diagram 3

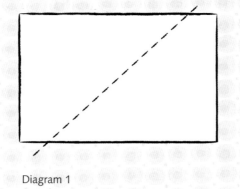

Diagram 1

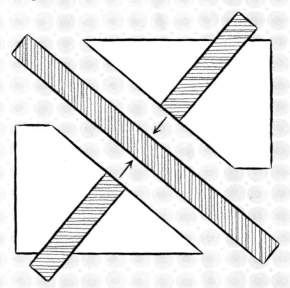

Diagram 4

Fence post border

18 Sew five fence post blocks together along the short sides to make a pieced fence post border strip. Press the seams. Make four sets of five blocks in this way.

19 Use the same pinning technique as for the inner border and sew a pieced fence post border strip to the top edge and another to the bottom edge of the quilt top. Press the seams toward the inner border.

20 Sew one 3½ in. (9 cm) gray print square to each end of the two remaining pieced fence post border strips.

21 Pin and then sew these pieced fence post border strips to the side edges of the quilt top. Press the seams toward the inner border.

Backing, quilting, and binding

22 Using the rotary cutter, mat, and ruler, square the quilt top if necessary.

23 Layer the backing, batting (wadding), and quilt top, following the instructions on page 100.

24 Quilt by machine or by hand as desired.

25 Bind the quilt, following the instructions on page 104.

Quilt layout

Drawn Together *by Sarah*

I love star patterns, and was particularly attracted to this one when I drew it. I like the columns of triangles, and the way the points form a circle without being curved. Multiples of these blocks would make a wonderful large quilt if sewn together and I would also like to try a larger star with more triangles working away from the center—one day!

Finished size

17¼ x 15¼ in. (44.6 x 39 cm)

Note Seams are stitched with right sides together using a ¼ in. (6 mm) seam allowance unless otherwise stated.

Material requirements

- 2 in. (5 cm) pink print fabric for piece 1
- 2 in. (5 cm) yellow-and-green print fabric for pieces 2 and 3
- 3 in. (7.5 cm) bright blue print fabric for piece 4
- 6 in. (15 cm) light blue-and-white fabric for pieces 5 and 6
- 10 in. (25.5 cm) purple print fabric for piece 7
- 12 in. (30.5 cm) solid white fabric for pieces 8 and 9
- 2 in. (5 cm) text print fabric for border
- 6 in. (15 cm) blue-and-white striped fabric for binding
- 19 x 22 in. (48 x 56 cm) backing fabric
- 19 x 22 in. (48 x 56 cm) cotton batting (wadding)
- Papers for foundation piecing (see page 99)
- Scissors for cutting paper
- Cotton thread for piecing
- Crewel embroidery no. 9 needles for hand quilting
- Blue and orange perle cotton for hand quilting
- Rotary cutter, mat, and ruler
- Sewing machine
- General sewing supplies

Cutting

From the pink print fabric, cut:
- Eight 2 x 3 in. (5 x 7.5 cm) rectangles (piece 1)

From the yellow-and-green print fabric, cut:
- Sixteen 2 x 2½ in. (5 x 6.5 cm) rectangles (pieces 2 and 3)

From the bright blue print fabric, cut:
- Eight 3 in. (7.5 cm) squares (piece 4)

From the light blue-and-white fabric, cut:
- Sixteen 3 in. (7.5 cm) squares (pieces 5 and 6)

From the purple print fabric, cut:
- Eight 4½ x 6 in. (11.5 x 15 cm) rectangles (piece 7)

From the solid white fabric, cut:
- Eight 6 in. (15 cm) squares
- Eight 4 x 4½ in. (10 x 11.5 cm) rectangles

From the text print border fabric, cut:
- One 1½ in.- (4 cm-) wide strip—cross-cut to yield two 1½ x 15¼ in. (4 x 39 cm) strips

From the blue-and-white striped binding fabric, cut:
- Two 3 in.- (7.5 cm-) wide strips

Foundation piecing

1 Following the instructions on page 9, copy foundation piecing patterns A and B on pages 112–113 onto four foundation papers each. (The two patterns are mirror images of each other.) The numbers on the patterns refer to the pieces, which correspond to the sewing order. Cut out the patterns, just outside the outer lines.

2 Sort the fabric pieces into sets for each unit. Make four each of A and B units, following the instructions for foundation piecing on page 99.

Assembly

3 Arrange the star pieces on a flat surface. Place one A and one B unit with right sides together, to make a square shape. Pin through the corners at the ¼ in. (6 mm) mark to line them up. Make sure all the points are matched—use extra pins if necessary.

4 Sew along the diagonal seam line, stitching with the paper side on top. Press the seam open from the back, and then from the front. Make four A/B square units.

5 Sew the units together in pairs and then sew the pairs together. Press.

6 Trim the block to measure 15¼ in. (39 cm) square, or to ¼ in. (6 mm) outside the star points.

7 Carefully remove all papers by tearing along the seam lines. Use tweezers or a pin to remove any small pieces from the seams.

8 Sew a 1½ x 15¼ in. (4 x 39 cm) text fabric strip to opposite sides of the star and press the seams toward the border.

Backing, quilting, and binding

9 Layer the backing, batting (wadding), and quilt top, following the instructions on page 100.

10 Using blue and orange perle cotton, hand quilt around the stars, following the instructions on page 102.

11 Using the rotary cutter, mat, and ruler, square the quilt top if necessary.

12 Bind the quilt, following the instructions on page 104.

Cocktail Shakers *by Amy*

Oh, this little quilt makes me squeal with delight! I would like to see this block tumble all the way down a quilt in a rainbow of colors. Cocktail Shakers is foundation pieced on papers for accuracy. Cheery shot cottons add depth and sparkle to this charmer.

Finished size

21 x 24 in. (53.5 x 61 cm)

Note Seams are stitched with right sides together using a ¼ in. (6 mm) seam allowance unless otherwise stated.

Material requirements

• ½ yd (45 cm) light purple fabric for background and borders

• 2 in.- (5 cm-) wide strip each of 16 different colored fabrics for blocks

• 3 in. (7.5 cm) green fabric for border

• ¼ yd (25 cm) striped fabric for binding

• 25 x 28 in. (63.5 x 71 cm) backing fabric

• 25 x 28 in. (63.5 x 71 cm) batting (wadding)

• Papers for foundation piecing (see page 99)

• Scissors for cutting paper

• Pale purple cotton thread for piecing and machine quilting

• Rotary cutter, mat, and ruler

• Sewing machine

• General sewing supplies

Cutting

From the light purple background and borders fabric, cut:

• Thirty-two 2 x 5½ in. (5 x 14 cm) rectangles

• Two 1¼ in.- (3 cm-) wide strips

• Two 2½ in.- (6.5 cm-) wide strips

From the 16 different colored fabrics, cut:

• Five 2 x 5½ in. (5 x 14 cm) rectangles each (80 in total)

From the green fabric, cut:

• Two 1¼ in.- (3 cm-) wide strips

From the striped binding fabric, cut:

• Three 2¼ in.- (6 cm-) wide strips

Foundation piecing

1 Following the instructions on page 99, copy the foundation piecing pattern from page 115 onto 16 foundation papers. The numbers on the pattern indicate the sewing order.

2 Sort the 80 different colored 2 x 5½ in. (5 x 14 cm) rectangles into sets for each block. A block uses three rectangles of one color, two of a contrasting color, and two of the light purple background fabric. Make 16 blocks, following the instructions for foundation piecing on page 99. Do not remove the papers.

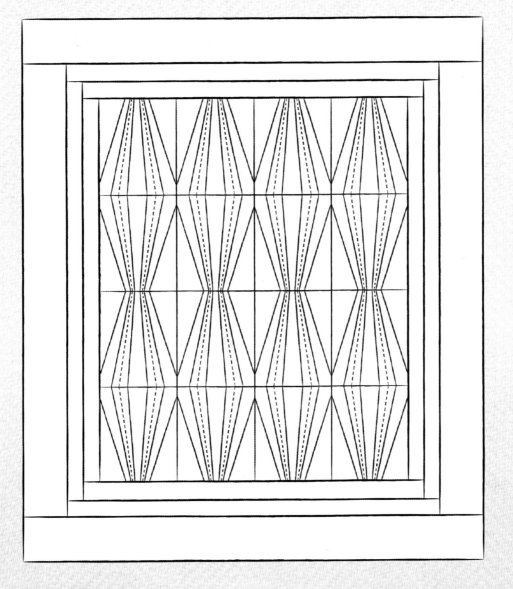

Assembly

3 Referring to the quilt layout, arrange the 16 blocks in four rows of four blocks.

4 Sew the blocks into four rows, ensuring they are aligned correctly. It is easiest to start sewing the blocks at the corners with the different colored fabrics, rather than from the corners with the background color.

5 Remove only the foundation paper that is in the seams and adjacent to the seams—do not remove the paper inside each block yet. Press the seams open.

6 Sew the rows together, ensuring the blocks are aligned correctly. Pinning the rows at color intersections will help keep the blocks in place while stitching.

7 Remove the rest of the foundation papers and press the seams open.

Borders

8 Measure down the quilt top through the center to get the true measurement. Cut two 1¼ in.- (3 cm-) wide light purple background strips to this measurement for the inner side borders. Fold the border strips in half, end to end, and mark the centers with pins. Mark the sides of the quilt top in the same way. Matching the pins and with right sides together, pin the two border strips to the side edges of the quilt top; stitch. Press the seams toward the border.

9 Measure across the quilt top through the center to get the true measurement. Cut two 1¼ in.- (3 cm-) wide light purple background strips to this measurement for the top and bottom inner borders. In the same way as in step 8, pin and then sew the light purple border strips to the top and bottom edges of the quilt top. Press the seams toward the border.

10 For the middle border, measure, cut, pin, and then sew 1¼ in.- (3 cm-) wide green strips to the side edges of the quilt top, in the same way as in step 8. Press the seams toward the middle border. Repeat for the top and bottom middle borders.

11 For the outer side border, measure, cut, pin, and then sew 2½ in.- (6.5 cm-) wide light purple border strips to the side edges of the quilt top, in the same way as in step 8. Press the seams toward the outer border. Repeat for the top and bottom outer borders.

Backing, quilting, and binding

12 Using the rotary cutter, mat, and ruler, square the quilt top if necessary.

13 Layer the backing, batting (wadding), and quilt top, following the instructions on page 100.

14 Using light purple cotton thread, machine quilt along the center of the second and fourth pieces in each block, following a path up and down the blocks. Outline quilt ¼ in. (6 mm) outside the edges of the colored blocks to form diamond shapes. Finally, quilt along the center of the inner and middle borders, and ½ in. (1.2 cm) from the seam on the outer border.

15 Bind the quilt, following the instructions on page 104.

Garden Paths *by Sarah*

Pretty garden paths wind through this little quilt, the block for which could also be used to create a wonderful larger quilt. The secondary patterns that are created where blocks join allow negative space to showcase your quilting.

Finished size

20½ in. (51.2 cm) square

Note Seams are stitched with right sides together using a ¼ in. (6 mm) seam allowance unless otherwise stated.

Material requirements

- 9 in. (23 cm) gray linen for background
- 3 in. (7.5 cm) each of three yellow fabrics for squares
- 3 in. (7.5 cm) small-scale blue floral fabric for diamonds
- 5 in. (13 cm) large-scale blue floral fabric for center square
- 6 in. (15 cm) striped fabric for border
- ⅓ yd (30 cm) blue-and-white fabric for binding
- 26 in. (66 cm) square of backing fabric
- 26 in. (66 cm) square of cotton batting (wadding)
- Crewel embroidery no. 9 needles for hand quilting
- Blue and orange perle 8 cotton for hand quilting
- Cotton thread for piecing
- Rotary cutter, mat, and ruler
- Sewing machine
- General sewing supplies

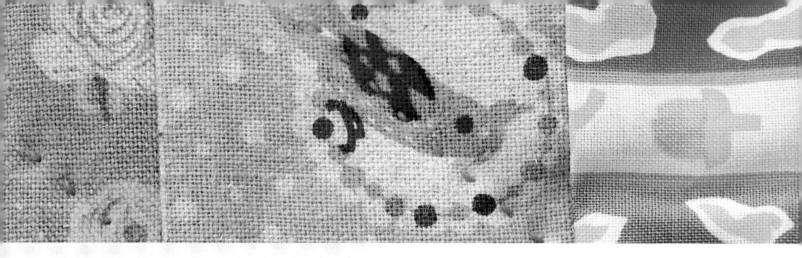

Cutting

From the gray linen background fabric, cut:

• Two 2½ in.- (6.2 cm-) wide strips. From these strips cut twelve 2½ in. (6.2 cm) squares and eight 4½ x 2½ in. (11.2 x 6.2 cm) rectangles.

• One 2⅞ in.- (7.2 cm-) wide strip. From this strip cut twelve 2⅞ in. (7.2 cm) squares. Cross-cut the squares on one diagonal to yield 24 half-square triangles.

From each of the three yellow fabrics, cut:

• Four 2½ in. (6.2 cm) squares, cutting the four that will be nearest the center from yellow A, the four that will be nearest the outer edge from yellow C, and the four that will be in between them from yellow B—see quilt photograph.

From the small-scale blue floral fabric, cut:

• One 2½ in.- (6.2 cm-) wide strip. Fold the strip in half, end to end, so the selvages are together. Using the 45-degree angle on the ruler, cross-cut the strip into four pairs of diamond shapes with 4½ in.- (11.2 cm-) long sides. Cutting the folded strip allows four diamonds to face one way and four the other way.

From the large-scale blue floral fabric, cut:

• One 4½ in. (11.2 cm) square.

From the striped fabric, cut:

• Two 2½ in.- (6.2 cm-) wide strips. Cut each strip in half to make four strips, each 2½ in. (6.2 cm) wide and as long as half of the fabric width.

From the blue-and-white binding fabric, cut:

• Three 3 in. (7.5 cm) strips.

Sewing

1 Sew a gray half-square triangle to each end of four small-scale blue floral diamonds to form a rectangle unit (see Diagram 1). Trim the "ears" off the triangles.

2 Sew a gray half-square triangle to each end of the remaining small-scale blue floral diamonds to form rectangle units (see Diagram 2) that are the mirror image of those in step 1. Trim the "ears."

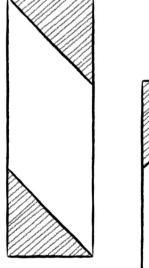

Diagram 1

Diagram 2

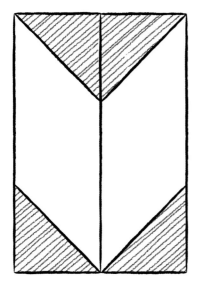

Diagram 3

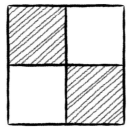

Diagram 4

3 Sew the eight units into pairs, matching up the opposite-facing diamonds to form a "V" (see Diagram 3).

4 Sew a gray 2½ in. (6.2 cm) square to each of the four yellow A squares. Repeat with the yellow B squares. Sew two units together to form a four-patch (see Diagram 4).

5 Sew one of the 2½ in. (6.2 cm) yellow C squares to one end of a gray rectangle (see Diagram 5). Make four.

6 Referring to the quilt photograph for correct placement, sew a gray rectangle to one side of the four-patch unit (see Diagram 6).

7 Check again for correct placement, and then sew the unit from step 5 to the side of the four-patch unit (see Diagram 7). Press. Make four units in this way.

8 Referring to the quilt photograph for correct placement, sew one of these units to a diamond unit from step 3, taking care to match the points. Sew another one of these units to the other side of the diamond unit (see Diagram 8). Make two of these rows.

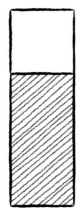

Diagram 5

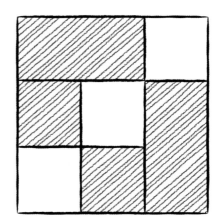

Diagram 6

Diagram 7

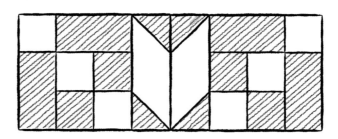

Diagram 8

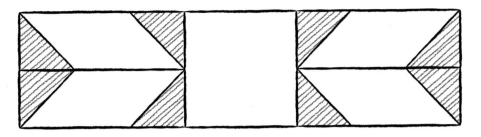

Diagram 9

Diagram 10

Diagram 11

9 Sew the remaining two diamond units to either side of the large blue floral square (see Diagram 9).

10 Referring to the quilt photograph, sew the three rows together to form the center of the quilt top.

Border

11 Fold each of the four 2½ in.- (6.2 cm-) wide striped strips in half, end to end, with right sides together. Make a 45-degree angle cut at the folded end of each strip. When you separate the two halves of a strip, you will have two pieces with facing 45-degree angles (see Diagram 10).

12 Sew a gray half-square triangle to the angled end of a strip. Make eight.

13 Sew a pair of facing triangle strips together at the gray triangle ends (see Diagram 11). Make four and then press.

14 Measure the quilt top through the center to get the true measurement. It should measure 16½ in. (41.2 cm) square. Cut the border strips to the size of the quilt top, ensuring the seam is in the center of each strip.

15 With right sides together, pin a border strip to the top edge and another to the bottom edge of the quilt top, matching the center seam of each border strip to that of the quilt top. Sew these borders to the quilt top (see page 100). Press the seams.

16 Sew a 2½ in. (6.2 cm) gray square to each end of the remaining two border strips. In the same way as in step 15, pin and then sew the borders to the side edges of the quilt top. Press the seams.

Backing, quilting, and binding

17 Using the rotary cutter, mat, and ruler, square the quilt top if necessary.

18 Layer the backing, batting (wadding), and quilt top, following the instructions on page 100.

19 Using perle 8 cotton thread, hand quilt around the shapes, following the instructions on page 102.

20 Bind the quilt, following the instructions on page 104.

Fans of May *by Amy*

I'm a big fan of May—I was born in May, was married in May, and celebrate Mother's Day in May. It's my favorite month! Fans of May evokes this time of year with light, pretty colors for the simple pieced center and border of dimensional fans. The curved corners echo the curved edges of the fans and add a touch of fun without a lot of fuss.

Finished size

16½ x 20½ in. (42 x 52 cm)

Note Seams are stitched with right sides together using a ¼ in. (6 mm) seam allowance unless otherwise stated.

Material requirements

• ½ yd (50 cm) assorted light pink, light aqua, light gray, and yellow fabric pieces for quilt center and fans—the pieces should be at least 2½ in. (6.5 cm) square and approximately equal in color value.

• ⅛ yd (15 cm) light pink print fabric for setting triangles

• 5 x 6 in. (13 x 15 cm) each of gold and red woolen fabrics

• 5 x 9 in. (13 x 23 cm) each of pink and aqua woolen fabrics

• ⅓ yd (30 cm) light aqua striped fabric for borders

• One fat quarter of yellow fabric for binding

• 2 yd (1.9 m) of ½ in.- (1.2 cm-) wide yellow rickrack

• 20 x 24 in. (51 x 61 cm) backing fabric

• 20 x 24 in. (51 x 61 cm) cotton batting (wadding)

• Template plastic (see page 116 for templates)

• Pencil for drawing on template plastic

• Scissors for cutting template plastic

• Papers for foundation piecing (see page 99)

• Scissors for cutting paper

• Neutral-colored cotton thread for piecing and machine appliqué

• White thread for machine quilting

• Rotary cutter, mat, and ruler

• Sewing machine

• General sewing supplies

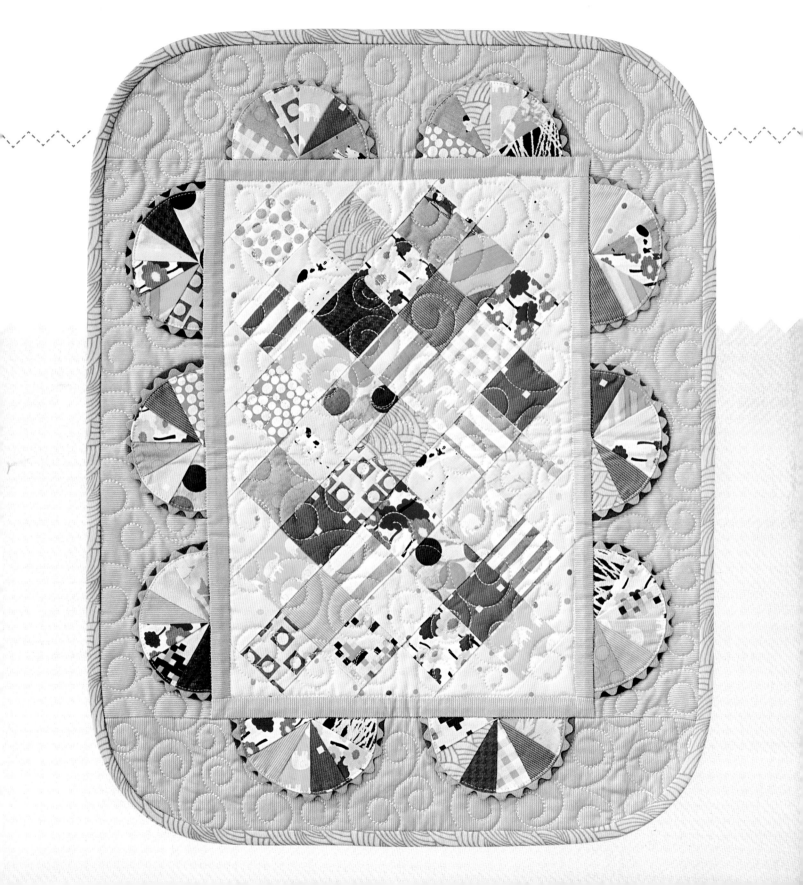

Sewing

1 Arrange the thirty-nine 2 in. (5 cm) assorted light pink, light aqua, light gray, and yellow fabric squares on point in rows (see Diagram 1).

2 Place the light pink quarter-square triangles around the outside of the squares, ensuring they are oriented correctly. Place the light pink half-square triangles at the corners (see Diagram 2). The triangles are purposely oversized so that the pieced center of the quilt will appear to float slightly on the light pink background fabric.

Cutting

From the template plastic:

• One each Templates A and B

From the assorted light pink, light aqua, light gray, and yellow fabrics, cut:

• Thirty-nine 2 in. (5 cm) squares

• Sixty 1½ x 2½ in. (4 x 6.5 cm) rectangles

From the light pink print fabric, cut:

• Four 4 in. (10 cm) squares—cross-cut each square on both diagonals to yield 16 quarter-square triangles.

• Two 3½ in. (9 cm) squares—cross-cut each square on one diagonal to yield four half-square triangles.

From each of the gold and red woolen fabrics, cut:

• Two Template A

From each of the pink and aqua woolen fabrics, cut:

• Three Template A

From the light aqua striped border fabric, cut:

• Two 1 in.- (2.5 cm-) wide strips for inner borders

• Two 3½ in.- (9 cm-) wide strips for outer borders

From the yellow binding fabric, cut:

• 2¼ in.- (6 cm-) wide bias strips to equal 70 in. (178 cm) following the instructions on page 105.

Diagram 1

Diagram 2

3 Sew the squares and quarter-square triangles into diagonal rows. Press each row, alternating the direction of the seams. Trim the corner "ears" off the triangles.

4 Sew the rows together, matching and pinning seams so the sewn intersections will meet neatly. Press the row seams.

5 Sew the light pink half-square triangles to the corners and press the quilt top. Trim the outside of the corner triangles so they line up with the top and side edges.

6 Trim the straight sides of the quilt top so that there is ½ in. (1.2 cm) of light pink background beyond the points of the outer pieced squares (see Diagram 3).

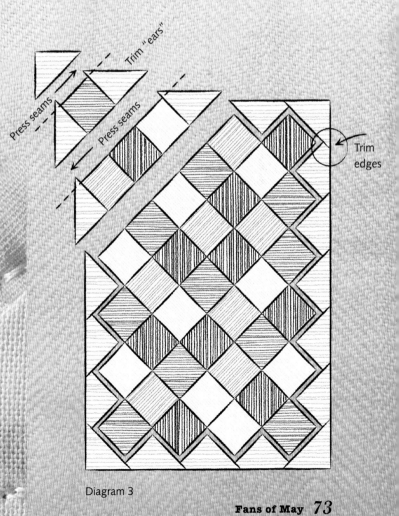

Diagram 3

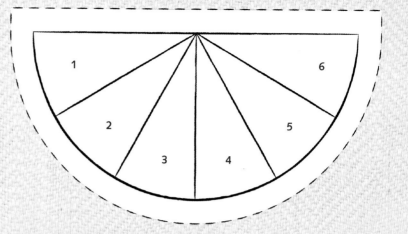

Foundation-pieced fans border

7 Following the instructions on page 99, copy the foundation piecing pattern on page 116 onto 10 foundation papers. (The numbers on the pattern indicate the order of sewing—see above.)

8 Sort the 60 light pink, light aqua, light gray, and yellow rectangles into sets of six pieces for each block. Make 10 blocks, following the instructions for foundation piecing on page 99. Carefully remove all papers.

Rickrack trim

9 Cut the rickrack into ten 7 in. (18 cm) pieces. Starting at the bottom of the curve on the fan, place a piece of rickrack on the right side of the fabric along the curved raw edge. Keeping the outer rickrack bumps even with the raw edge, stitch down the center of the rickrack along the curved edge. Press the seam flat.

10 Turn the rickrack to the back of the pieced half circle so that the points extend beyond the edge; press. Repeat with the remaining fans.

Appliqué

11 Arrange the 10 foundation-pieced fans and the 10 woolen Template A half-circles around the quilt top with two at the top, two at the bottom, and three at each side, so that the colors are distributed around the quilt top.

12 Center a fan on top of a half-circle, aligning the straight edges. Stitch the fan in place ⅛ in. (3 mm) inside the finished curved edge, leaving the rickrack free. Repeat for the remaining fans and half-circles.

Use a digital camera to take a photo of your arrangement. This will help if you rearrange the pieces later for sewing.

Borders

13 Measure down the quilt top through the center to get the true measurement. Cut a strip to this length from each of the two 1 in.- (2.5 cm-) wide light aqua striped strips for the side inner borders. Fold the border strips in half, end to end, and mark the centers with pins. Mark the sides of the quilt top in the same way. Matching the pins and with right sides together, pin the inner borders to the sides of the quilt top; sew in place. Press the seams toward the border.

14 For the top and bottom inner borders, measure across the quilt top through the center to get the true measurement, and cut the remaining portions of the two 1 in.- (2.5 cm-) wide striped strips to this measurement. Pin and then sew the inner borders to the top and bottom of the quilt top in the same way as in step 13, again pressing the seams toward the border.

15 Measure and cut outer border strips for the sides of the quilt top from the two 3½ in.- (9 cm-) wide light aqua striped strips, as in step 13. Fold the strips in half, end to end, and then in half again; press the folds. Center three fans, right side up, over the creases on the right side of each strip, aligning the straight edges of the fans with the raw edge of the border strip. Baste (tack) the fans in place. Pin and then sew the side borders to the side inner borders. Press the seam toward the inner border.

16 In the same way as in step 13, measure and cut the top and bottom outer borders from the remaining portions of the two 3½ in.- (9 cm-) wide striped strips, fold in half, and press. Place these strips along the top and bottom of the quilt and center two fans on each strip. Baste (tack) the fans in place. Pin and then sew the top and bottom outer borders to the inner borders. Press the seam toward the inner border.

Backing, quilting, and binding

17 Layer the backing, batting (wadding), and quilt top, following the instructions on page 100.

18 Stitch around the quilt center along the edge of the pink background to stabilize the quilt. Quilt an all-over swirl motif over the center of the quilt and the borders (see Diagram 14, page 103.

Hold each fan away from the border when quilting nearby. The fans should stand away from the surface of the quilt.

19 Using the rotary cutter, mat, and ruler, square the quilt top if necessary.

20 Place Template B on the quilt top, just inside the corner (see Diagram 4). Draw around the curve with a pencil and then cut the quilt top along the drawn line. Repeat for the other corners.

21 Bind the quilt with the bias binding, following the instructions on page 105.

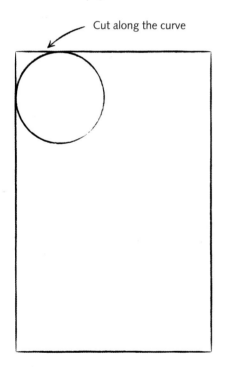

Cut along the curve

Diagram 4

Honeycomb *by Sarah*

This quilt is as cute as a button! Combining hand piecing with my love of embroidery, this is a wonderful carry-around project. It would look beautiful displayed on a wall or made into a little oval cushion for your bed.

Finished size

10 x 13½ in. (25.5 x 34.5 cm)

Note Seams are stitched with right sides together using a ¼ in. (6 mm) seam allowance unless otherwise stated.

Material requirements

• At least twelve 4½ in. (11.5 cm) squares of vintage sheeting or floral fabrics for background

• One fat quarter of purple-and-white striped fabric for binding

• 13 x 17 in. (33 x 43 cm) backing fabric

• 13 x 17 in. (33 x 43 cm) cotton batting (wadding)

• 2B pencil

• Heavy paper or pre-cut 2 in. (5 cm) English paper piecing hexagon papers

• Template plastic (see pages 117 and 119 for templates)

• Scissors for cutting template plastic

• Fine milliners needles for hand stitching

• Neutral-colored cotton thread for hand stitching

• Black and yellow Aurifil Cotton 50 cotton thread

• Crewel embroidery needles no. 9 for hand quilting and embroidery

• Variegated light blue perle 8 cotton for hand quilting

• Small embroidery hoop

• Basting spray, optional

• Black felt-tipped marker and one sheet of paper

• Light box or masking tape

• Rotary cutter, mat, and ruler

• Sewing machine

• General sewing supplies

Cutting

From template plastic, cut:

• One Template A (hexagon)

• One Template N (oval) from Paper Dolls

From the vintage sheeting squares or floral fabrics, cut:

• Ten whole hexagons—trace around Template A on the wrong side of the fabric with a pencil and then cut ¼ in. (6 mm) outside the drawn line.

• Eight partial hexagons—trace and cut as for whole hexagons, but using only the corners of Template A.

From the heavy paper (if not using precut papers), cut:

• Ten whole hexagons using Template A

• Eight half or partial hexagons using a portion of Template A

From the binding fabric, cut:

• 3 in.- (7.5 cm-) wide bias strips to equal 40 in. (102 cm), following the instructions on page 105

Hexagons

1 Place a fabric hexagon right side down. Place a paper hexagon on top. There should be ¼ in. (6 mm) fabric all around the paper (see Diagram 1).

2 Fold the fabric edges over the paper, mitering the corners. Sew through the paper and the fabric using large running stitches near the edge of the paper, being sure to anchor the corners. When you have stitched all the way around, fasten off the thread (see Diagram 2). Make ten hexagons and eight partial hexagons.

There are various ways to baste hexagons to the papers for English paper piecing. You can glue them with paper glue or use binding clips to hold them in place while you stitch. However, sewing the fabric in place, as in step 2, means that everything is safe and solid, it makes removing the papers easy, and also allows the papers to be reused afterward.

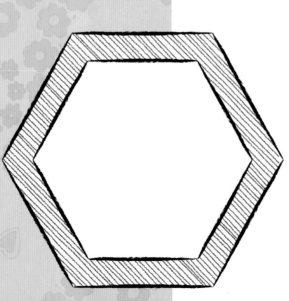

Diagram 1

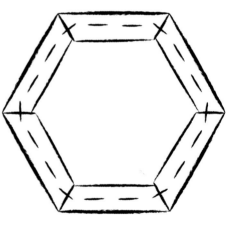

Diagram 2

3 Lay out the hexagons and decide where you want to place the colors. There are four whole hexagons down the center of the quilt, three whole hexagons on each side of the center, and eight partial hexagons to fill in around them (see Diagram 3—the arrows indicate where the small filler pieces should go).

4 Pick up two hexagons and place them with right sides together. Using a fine milliners needle and neutral-colored thread, whipstitch along the top of the hexagons, catching just the fabric and not the paper (see Diagrams 4 and 5).

5 Sew another hexagon to these two hexagons in the same manner (see Diagram 6—the arrow indicates where it will go). Sew all the hexagons together in the same way, following the layout in Diagram 3. Press.

6 Carefully remove the running stitches and the papers from the quilt top.

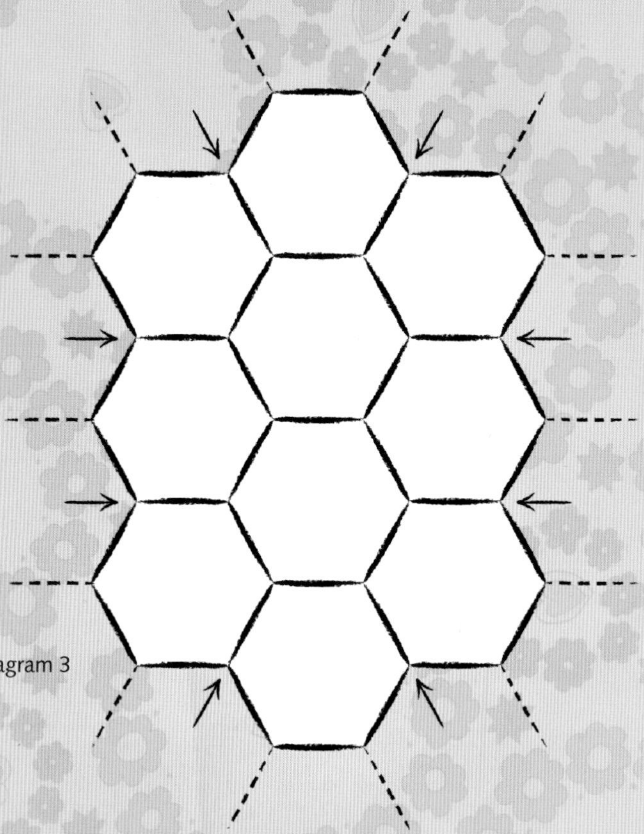

Diagram 3

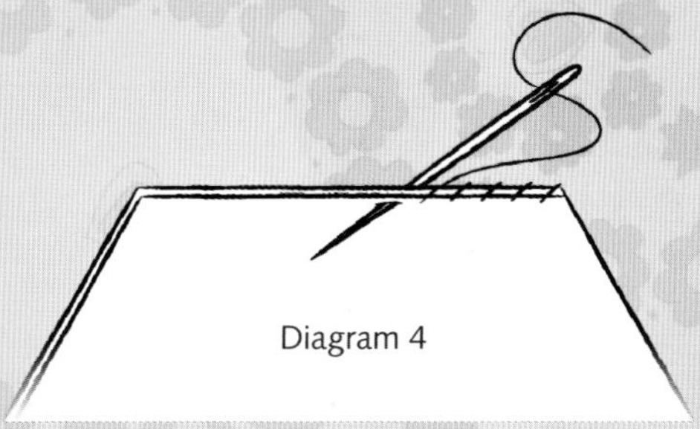

Diagram 4

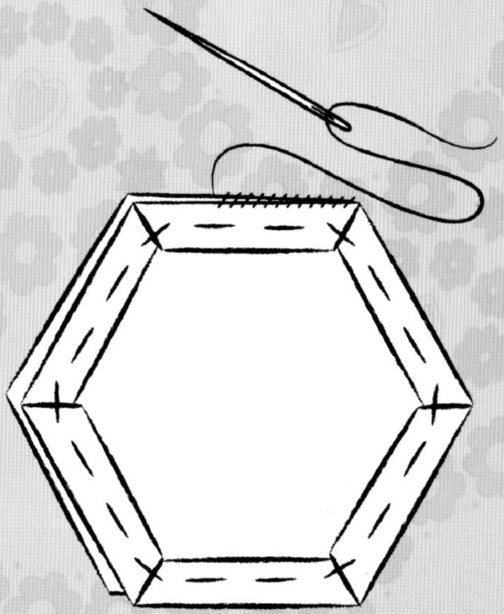

Diagram 5

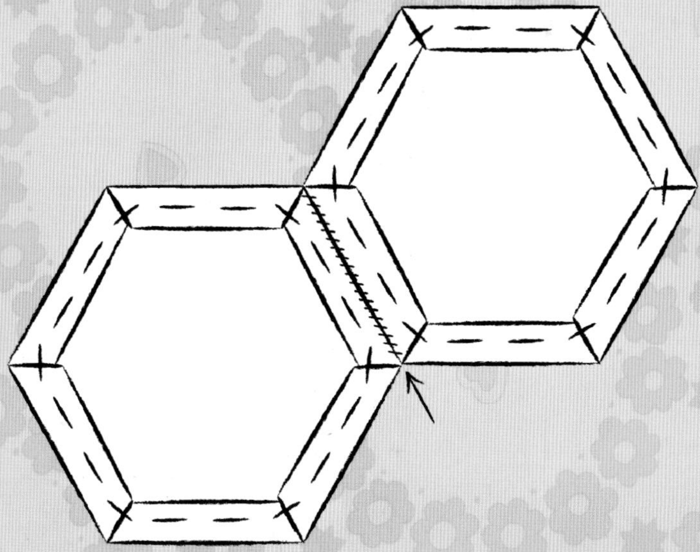

Diagram 6

Embroidery

7 Using a window or a light box, trace Template B (bee) onto the right side of the pieced hexagons using a 2B pencil. (To do this, trace it first onto paper with a black felt-tipped marker, then tape the paper to the window or place it on a light box. Place the fabric on top, right side up, and if using a window, tape this in place too, then trace the outline with the 2B pencil.)

8 Baste (tack) the hexagons onto the batting (wadding) only—not the backing fabric. You can either use basting spray, which means that there will be no basting stitches to get in the way of the embroidery, or baste with running stitches.

9 The bee is embroidered through the batting as well as the fabric for a full, textured look, using one strand of Aurifil Cotton 50 cotton thread and a crewel embroidery needle. Place in a hoop to ensure that you don't pucker the embroidery.

10 Using black thread, embroider the legs and eyes with satin stitch (see Diagram 7). Outline the wings, head, feelers, and body with backstitch (see Diagram 8). Fill in the head shape with seed stitch (see Diagram 9), and fill in the body with colonial knots (see Diagram 10).

11 Using black and yellow threads, fill in the abdomen with straight stitches a little way apart from one another in alternating bands.

12 Press the quilt face down on a towel to avoid flattening the embroidery.

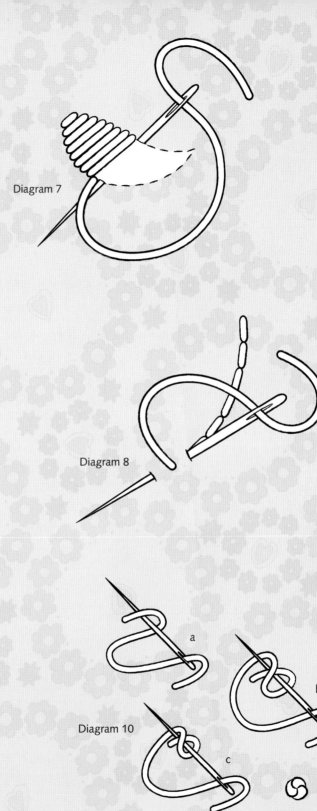

Diagram 7

Diagram 8

Diagram 10

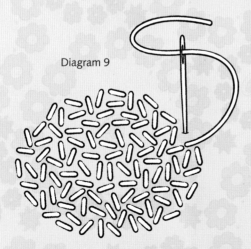

Diagram 9

Backing, quilting, and binding

13 Layer the backing, batting (wadding), and quilt top, following the instructions on page 100, remembering that the batting is already attached to the quilt top.

14 Using variegated light blue perle 8 cotton, hand quilt ¼ in. (6 mm) inside all the hexagons, avoiding the embroidered bee.

15 Fold the quilt in half crosswise, and finger press a crease. To draw the top left-hand quarter of the oval, line up the shorter straight edge of Template N with the crease. Using a pencil, trace the shape on the background. To draw the bottom left-hand quarter of the oval, flip the template, line it up again with the center crease, and trace the shape on the background. Flip the template again to do the other half of the oval in the same way. Carefully cut around the oval along the drawn line.

16 Bind the quilt with bias binding, following the instructions on page 105.

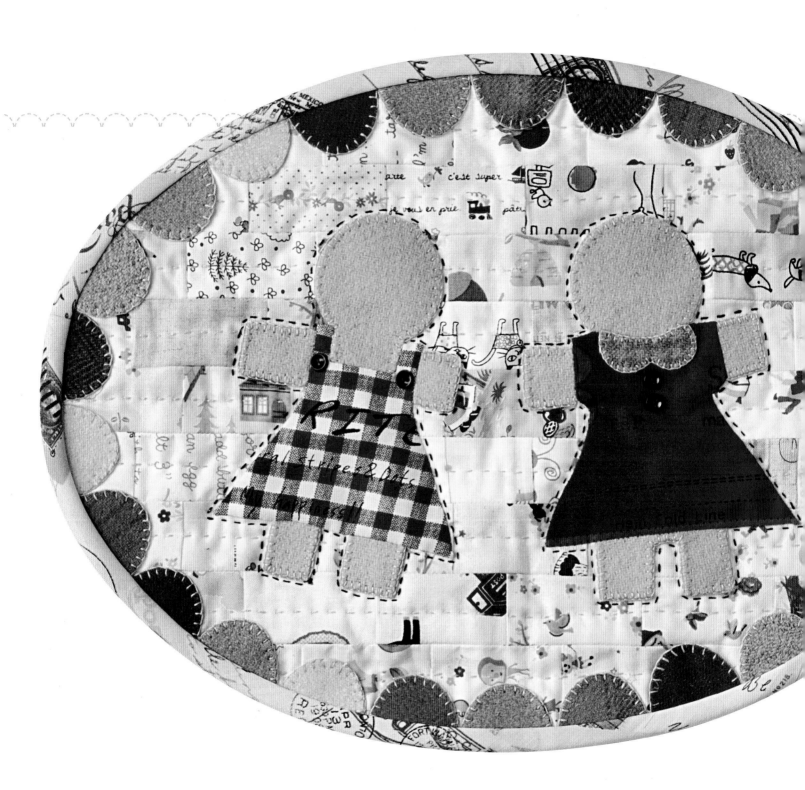

Paper Dolls *by Amy*

These dolls are very special as they were mascots for a dolly-quilt program that Sarah and I ran a few years ago. I released the dolls from their clothesline for this quilt, only to confine them to a fabric background. I love little projects with lots of details, so machine piecing, hand appliqué, and some embroidery all come into play in this project. The key word here is "play"!

Finished size

10 x 13½ in. (25.5 x 34.5 cm)

Note Seams are stitched with right sides together using a ¼ in. (6 mm) seam allowance unless otherwise stated.

Material requirements

• ¼ yd (25 cm) assorted cream and light print fabrics for the background—minimum size 2 x 3 in. (5 x 7.5 cm)

• 5 x 14 in. (13 x 35.5 cm) pink woolen fabric for dolls

• 1½ x 2½ in. (4 x 6.5 cm) woolen fabric scrap for doll dress collar

• Two 5 in. (13 cm) squares of print fabric for doll dresses

• ⅛ yd (15 cm) assorted woolen fabrics in blue, pink, green, and yellow for scallop border—minimum size 2 x 2½ in. (5 x 6.5 cm)

• Four ¼ in. (6 mm) black buttons

• One fat quarter of backing fabric

• 14 x 18 in. (35.5 x 45.5 cm) batting (wadding)

• One fat quarter of print fabric for binding

• Large sheet of template plastic (see pages 118–119 for templates)

• Pencil for tracing on template plastic

• Scissors for cutting template plastic

• Silver gel pen

• Cotton thread for piecing

• Appliqué needles

• Crewel embroidery no. 9 needles

• Tan and black perle 8 or 12 cotton for hand quilting and buttonhole stitching

• Appliqué glue

• Sewing machine

• General sewing supplies

Cutting

From the template plastic, cut:

• One each Templates A–F (Doll A)

• One each Templates G–L (Doll B)

• One Template M (border scallop)

• One Template N (portion of oval)

From the cream and light print fabrics, cut:

• Eighty-eight 1½ x 2½ in. (4 x 6.5 cm) rectangles

From the pink woolen fabric, cut:

• One each Templates A–E and G–J for dolls

From the woolen scrap fabric, cut:

• One Template L for doll dress collar for Doll B

From the two print fabrics, cut:

• One Template F from one and one Template K from the other—trace around each template on the right side of the fabric with the silver gel pen and then cut ¼ in. (6 mm) outside the drawn line for the needle-turn appliqué seam allowance.

From the blue, pink, green, and yellow woolen fabric, cut:

• 26 Template M

From the binding fabric, cut:

• 2¼ in.- (6 cm-) wide bias strips to equal 45 in. (115 cm) following the instructions on page 105.

Sewing

1 Sew eight 1½ x 2½ in. (4 x 6.5 cm) cream and light print fabric rectangles together along the short edges to make one strip (see Diagram 1). Press the seams open. Make 11 pieced strips.

2 Sew the strips together, offsetting the rows. Start the second row halfway along the first rectangle in the first row (see Diagram 2).

3 Fold the pieced background in half crosswise, and finger press a crease. To draw the top left-hand quarter of the oval, line up the shorter straight edge of Template N with the crease, near the top. Using a silver gel pen, trace the shape on the background. To draw the bottom left quarter of the oval, flip the template, line it up again with the center crease, and trace the shape on the background. Flip the template again to do the other half of the oval in the same way (see Diagram 3). Do not cut out the fabric oval.

4 Arrange the 26 woolen fabric Template M pieces around the edges of the oval with the straight raw edges of the woolen fabric even with the silver gel pen line (see Diagram 4). Using a small drop of appliqué glue in the center of each piece, attach the woolen pieces to the background.

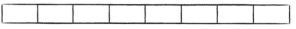

Diagram 1

Diagram 2

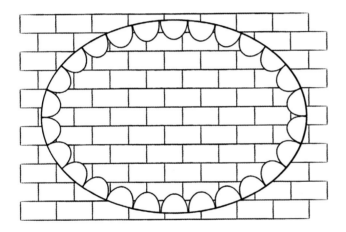

Diagram 3

Diagram 4

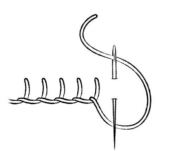

Diagram 5

5 Using the tan perle cotton thread and a crewel needle, buttonhole stitch around the curved edges of each piece to attach them to the background (see Diagram 5).

6 Arrange the pink woolen fabric doll body parts (Templates A–E and G–J) in the center of the oval. Check that each doll's dress will cover the inner edges of the body parts (see Diagram 6), and adjust the positions if necessary. Apply a small drop of appliqué glue to the center of each body part piece, and stick these pieces to the background. Using the tan perle cotton and a crewel needle, buttonhole stitch around the outer raw edges of the pieces—the inner raw edges will be covered by the dresses so do not need to be stitched.

7 Arrange the dolls' dresses (Templates F and K) to cover the inner unstitched edges of the body parts. Lift the edges of the dresses and place a dot of glue on the back of each dress, allowing enough space around the edge to turn under the seam allowance. Wait a few minutes for the glue to dry and then finger press the seam allowances under the edges of the dresses. Using a straw needle and thread to match the dress fabric, needle-turn appliqué the dresses to the background following the instructions on page 96.

8 Arrange the woolen collar (Template L) on the dress of Doll B. Using the tan perle cotton and a crewel needle, buttonhole stitch it in place.

9 Sew two ¼ in. (6 mm) black buttons on each dress with matching thread.

Diagram 6

Diagram 7

Diagram 8

Backing, quilting, and binding

10 Layer the backing, batting (wadding), and quilt top, following the instructions on page 100.

11 Using a crewel needle and tan perle cotton thread, hand quilt straight lines along the center of each long row of background rectangles, following the instructions on page 102. Change to black perle cotton and hand quilt around the doll shapes (see Diagram 7).

12 Trim the excess fabric, batting, and backing along the silver gel pen line forming the large oval (see Diagram 8).

13 Bind the quilt with the bias binding, following the instructions on page 105.

Cuttings *by Sarah and Amy*

You could almost say this was a mystery quilt—Sarah didn't quite know what she was getting in the mail, and Amy didn't know what Sarah would do with it! For this joint project, Sarah took Amy's finished pieced wheel and transformed it into a whimsical potted flower. This quilt features some favorite techniques: Sarah's hand appliqué and Amy's rickrack appliqué by machine.

Finished size

20 x 27 in. (51 x 68.8 cm)

Note Seams are stitched with right sides together using a ¼ in. (6 mm) seam allowance unless otherwise stated.

Material requirements

• 5 in. (13 cm) square each of 20 assorted print fabrics

• 3½ x 8 in. (9 x 20.5 cm) each of 10 assorted light print fabrics

• 20 in. (55 cm) salmon print fabric for background

• 6 in. (15 cm) green print fabric for leaves

• 6 in. (15 cm) square of peach print fabric for center circle

• 8 x 10 in. (20.5 x 25.5 cm) garden print fabric for flowerpot

• One fat quarter of green-and-white fabric for binding

• 24 x 30 in. (61 x 76 cm) backing fabric

• 24 x 30 in. (61 x 76 cm) batting (wadding)

• 2 yd (1.9 m) of ⅝ in.- (1.5 cm-) wide brown rickrack

• Cotton thread for piecing

• Two sheets template plastic (see pages 120–121 for templates)

• Pencil for tracing on template plastic

• Scissors to cut template plastic

• Silver gel pen

• Appliqué glue

• Appliqué needles

• Green cotton thread to match leaves

• Crewel embroidery no. 9 needles for hand quilting

• Pink and green Aurifil cotton 12 thread for hand quilting

• Rotary cutter, mat, and ruler

• Sewing machine

• General sewing supplies

Cutting

From the template plastic, cut:

• One Template A (wedge)

• One Template B (center circle)

• One Template C (leaf)

• One Template D (pot)

• One Template E (curved corner)

From the 20 assorted print fabrics, cut:

• Sixty 1½ x 5 in. (4 x 14 cm) rectangles

From the 10 assorted light print fabrics, cut:

• Ten Template A

From the salmon print fabric, cut:

• One 20 in. (51 cm) square

• Two 8 x 3 in. (20.5 x 7 cm) rectangles

• Two 5¾ x 7½ in. (14.7 x 19 cm) rectangles

From the green print fabric, cut:

• One 3½ x 1¼ in. (9 x 3 cm) rectangle

• One Template C and one reversed Template C—trace the template onto the right side of the fabric using the silver gel pen, and cut out each shape ¼ in. (6 mm) outside the silver gel line.

From the garden print fabric, cut:

• One 7½ x 9½ in. (19 x 24 cm) rectangle

From the peach print fabric, cut:

• One Template B

From the green-and-white binding fabric, cut:

• 3 in.- (7.5 cm-) wide bias strips to equal 95 in. (242 cm) in length—follow the instructions on page 105.

Pieced wedges

1 Sew six 1½ x 5 in. (4 x 13 cm) rectangles together along the long edges (see Diagram 1). Press the seams open. Make 10 sets.

2 From each of the 10 sets, cut one wedge using Template A (see Diagram 2).

3 Sew a pieced wedge to a light print wedge along the long edge (see Diagram 3). Press the seams open. Make 10 pairs.

4 Sew the wedge pairs together to form a circle (see Diagram 4).

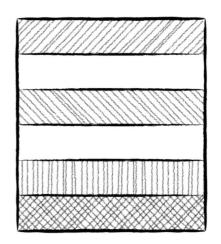

Diagram 1

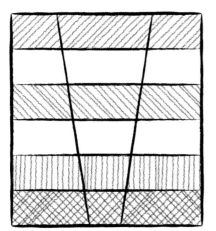

Diagram 2

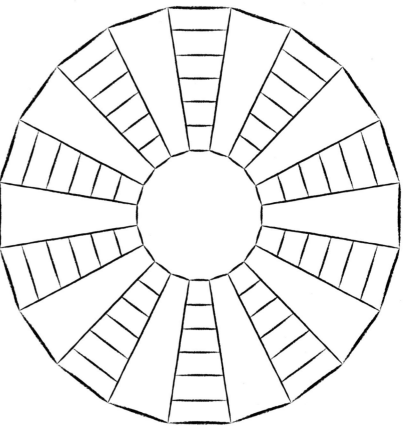

Diagram 4

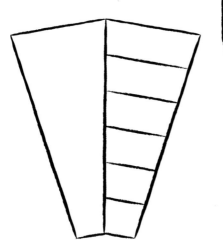

Diagram 3

Rickrack appliqué

5 Place a piece of rickrack along the raw edge of the pieced wedge circle, on the right side of the fabric. Leave approximately 1½ in. (4 cm) of rickrack free before starting to stitch.

6 Keeping the outer rickrack bumps even with the raw edge, stitch down the center of the rickrack along the curved edge (see Diagram 5).

7 When the stitching has almost reached the beginning, near the free end of the rickrack, fold up that end.

8 Continue to stitch toward the folded rickrack. Pause the stitching to place the raw end of the rickrack over the folded end and decide the best place to join them. Align the rickrack bumps as this will help hide the join.

9 Trim the excess rickrack at the beginning and end, and then complete the stitching through the overlapped layers (see Diagram 6). Press the seam and turn the rickrack to the back of the pieced circle, so that the bumps extend beyond the edge; press.

10 Fold the 20 in. (51 cm) salmon print square into quarters and finger-press.

11 Press under ¼ in. (6 mm) along the long edges of the 3½ x 1¼ in. (9 x 3 cm) green print rectangle for the stem.

12 Center the pieced circle on the salmon print background square using the finger-pressed creases as a guide. Tuck the end of the green stem under the circle at the center of the bottom of the block. Hold the pieces in place with a few drops of appliqué glue.

13 Stitch the pieced circle in place ⅛ in. (3 mm) inside the finished curved edge, leaving the rickrack and the stem free.

14 Stitch rickrack around the peach print Template B circle in the same way as in steps 5–9. Center this circle over the pieced circle and stitch ⅛ in. (3 mm) inside the Template B circle, leaving the rickrack free.

Leaf appliqué

15 Referring to the quilt photograph, position the two leaves on the salmon background fabric. Tuck the bottom edges of the leaves under the stem. The tops of the leaves will be approximately ¾ in. (2 cm) from the edge of the background square. Hold the pieces in place with a few drops of appliqué glue.

16 Finger-press around the edges of the leaves and then needle-turn appliqué the leaves and the stem with green thread, following the instructions on page 96.

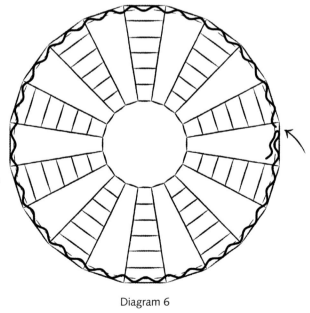

To see step-by-step photographs of this technique, visit the tutorial on Amy's blog, http://mrsschmenkmanquilts.wordpress.com/tutorial-ric-rac-applique/

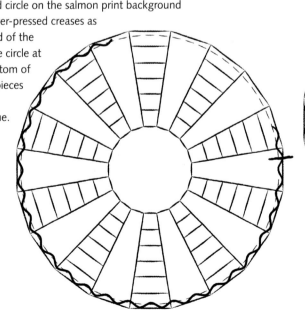

Diagram 5

Diagram 6

Assembly

17 Place Template D on the 9½ x 7½ in. (24 x 19 cm) garden print rectangle and cut along the angled edge to make the pot shape (see Diagram 7). Flip the template over and repeat on the other side of the rectangle (see Diagram 8).

18 Sew a 3 x 8 in. (7 x 20.5 cm) salmon print rectangle on each side of the pot, with the rectangles extending a little at the top and bottom of the pot (see Diagram 9). Open out and press the seams toward the pot.

19 Trim the extra fabric so that the rectangle measures 9½ x 7½ in. (24 x 19 cm). Sew a 5¾ x 7½ in. (14.7 x 19 cm) salmon print rectangle to each side; press.

20 Sew the pot unit to the bottom of the flower-and-leaves unit and then press.

Backing, quilting, and binding

21 Layer the backing, batting (wadding), and quilt top, following the instructions on page 100.

22 Using green perle cotton, hand quilt around the outline of the leaves and pot and along the center of each wedge, following the instructions on page 1-2. Using pink perle cotton, hand quilt straight horizontal lines across the background, spacing them 1 in. (2.5 cm) apart.

23 Using the rotary cutter, mat, and ruler, square the quilt top if necessary. Place Template E just inside one corner of the quilt, and trim along the curved edge through all layers. Repeat for the other three corners.

24 Bind the quilt with the bias binding, following the instructions on page 105.

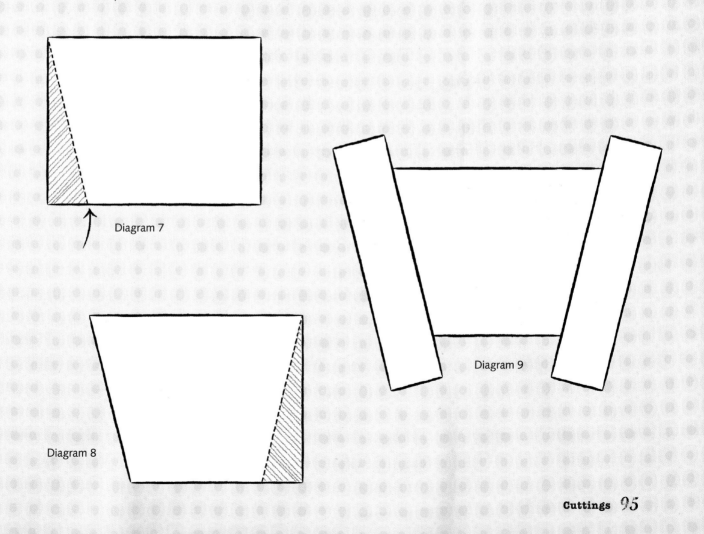

Diagram 7

Diagram 8

Diagram 9

Techniques

This section covers the basic techniques used in this book. You may be familiar with many of them, but there may be some that we approach a little differently than you are used to. Therefore it is important that you read the instructions carefully before starting your quilt.

Appliqué

There are various appliqué techniques, but Sarah's favorite is the needle-turn method, described here. Whatever method you choose, complete all the appliqué before you piece the blocks together, unless otherwise instructed.

Before beginning the appliqué, decide where you want your shapes to sit on the background block. Use a sharp 2B pencil or other marker to lightly trace the shapes onto the background fabric.

Remember that some designs need to have their elements sewn down in a particular order. For example, when sewing a flower, the stem needs to be sewn first so that it sits under the flower petals, then the petals are added, and finally the flower center and the leaves. If you are working on a complicated appliqué design and you think you might get confused, draw or photocopy a diagram of the complete design, determine the order in which the pieces need to be laid down, and then number the shapes on the diagram so that you can keep track.

Needle-turn appliqué

1 Using a sharp 2B pencil, trace the template shapes onto template plastic or cardstock. Using paper scissors (not your fabric scissors), cut out along the drawn line.

2 Place the template on the right side of the fabric and trace around it, taking care to leave space between the pieces for a seam allowance. Use a silver gel pen for marking sewing lines, first, because it's reflective and shows up on any fabric, and second, because it's really easy to see whether or not you have turned the shape under neatly or not. If you can still see silver, you haven't got the shape right! However, gel pen does not wash off. Once you have traced your shape onto the fabric, you're married to it, so be careful with that tracing!

3 Cut out the shapes a scant ¼ in. (6 mm) outside the gel line. Finger press along the line all around the shape, including into any curves or points (see Diagram 1). Do not be tempted to iron along the seam line. A finger-pressed line is easy to manipulate, while an ironed line is difficult to change if you iron a point into a crease or a line in the wrong spot. You will also be very likely to burn your fingers. Finger pressing is a guide to help you turn the fabric as you sew.

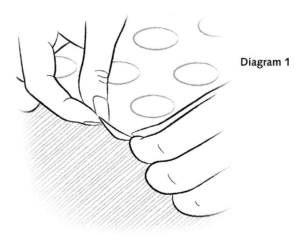

Diagram 1

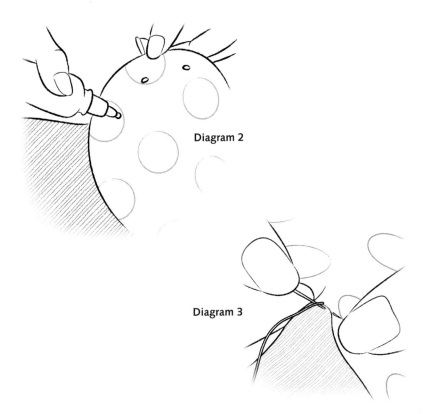

Diagram 2

Diagram 3

4 Position the pieces on the background block, using the traced outline or photograph supplied with the pattern as a guide. Note which parts of the pieces may go under others; dotted lines on the templates indicate which parts of each piece should be placed under adjacent pieces.

5 Instead of pins, use liquid appliqué glue (not a glue stick) to fix the pieces temporarily onto the background (see Diagram 2). You can glue all the appliqué shapes onto a quilt and carry it around with you, without worrying that the pins have come out. You only need a few dots of glue on each shape to make them stick. Leave for a few minutes for the glue to dry. Don't worry if the glue smudges, as it is easily peeled back later or washed off.

6 Thread an appliqué needle with thread to match the appliqué fabric. You should always match the appliqué thread to the color of the fabric shape that you are appliquéing, not to the background. Use a very long, fine straw needle for appliqué—the finer the needle, the smaller you can make your stitches for invisible appliqué. You can start anywhere, but try never to start on an inside curve.

7 Tie a knot in the thread and come up from the back to the front of the background fabric, catching the very edge of the appliqué shape with the needle (see Diagram 3).

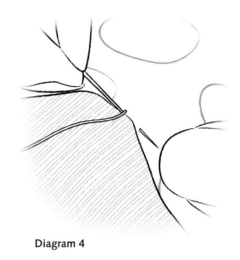

Diagram 4

Points and curves

Here is the best way to get a sharp point. Sew all the way up to the point on one side. Fold the fabric down 90 degrees under the point and then sweep the remaining fabric downward and underneath the main part of the point. Take a stitch right at the point again and give it a sharp tug, then continue sewing down the other side of the point.

When you get to an inside (concave) curve, you've reached your next challenge! You can sew all around the outside curves without clipping, but inside curves need clipping. Using very sharp, small scissors, carefully clip up to the silver line, about ¼ in. (6 mm) apart, all around the inner curve. Never clip anything until you are ready to sew it. If you do, the fabric can fray and get messy. Sew all the way up to the curve before you clip, and then sew the curve right away.

8 Go down into the background fabric right next to where you came up, run the needle along underneath the background, and come up again right on the edge of the appliqué shape (see Diagram 4). Don't try to turn the whole edge under before you sew it; just turn under the small section you are working on. This makes it easier to keep track of the gel pen line and make sure that you turn it all under.

9 Sew all around the cut edge of the appliqué shape in this manner. The stitches should just catch the edge of the fabric and be quite small and close together, which will make the appliqué strong and avoid its being torn or looking puckered. Continue until you have sewn all around the outside of the shape, and then tie the thread off at the back with a small knot.

10 Turn the block over and make a small cut at the back of the shape, taking care not to cut the appliqué. Cut away the background fabric underneath the appliqué. Be sure not to cut closer than ¼ in. (6 mm) from the seam lines. Although it is not necessary, removing the fabric in this way makes the appliqué sit nicely and creates fewer layers to quilt through, especially where appliqué pieces overlap. Repeat this process with each shape. Remove the background from under each piece before you apply the next one.

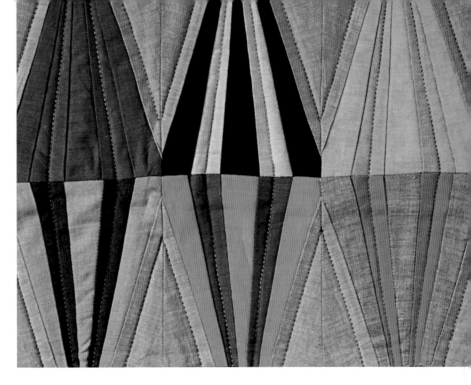

Foundation piecing

Foundation piecing is a clever technique used to make blocks of exactly the same size, to achieve accurate designs with sharp points, or to stabilize scraps and control bias stretching. It involves, as the name implies, the use of paper or fabric as a base, or foundation, for piecing. Lines drawn on the underside of the foundation allow straight, accurate seams that make it possible to sew even the most advanced blocks perfectly. The patterns are marked with the sewing order for piecing the fabrics.

Foundation papers can be purchased in quilt or craft shops. The block designs need to be traced or copied onto the papers, so you will need at least one page per block. If copying, ensure the copies are an accurate, 100 percent (same-size) reproduction. Be sure to choose a paper that feeds into your printer or photocopier. In some cases, it is possible to use standard copier paper, but if seams intersect, this is not such a good option. The paper is removed once the blocks are sewn and this task can be tedious if the paper cannot be removed easily.

1 Set your sewing machine to a small stitch—say, 1.5 (19 stitches per inch/2.5 cm on older machines)—which helps when the time comes to remove the papers. Sewing through the paper will dull the needle, so remember to change to a fresh needle when doing other sewing.

2 Place the first two fabrics with right sides together, with the paper right side up on top (see Diagram 5). Hold the paper up to a light to be sure that the fabric covers the necessary area. Be aware of where the fabric will be sewn and make sure that it will cover the next seam when pressed flat. Sew along the line between piece 1 and piece 2, trim the excess seam allowance, then flip the strip and press it in place. Be sure to leave a ¼ in. (6 mm) seam allowance on the last strip.

3 Continue to stitch the remaining fabrics in the correct order until all pieces are sewn (see Diagram 6).

4 When the block is completely stitched, trim it using a ruler and rotary cutter, making sure to include the seam allowance on all outside edges. Fold over the first strip at the seam and finger press along the sewing line. Use a seam ripper to gently help loosen the paper before pulling it away. Do not rip out the paper or the stitches will loosen.

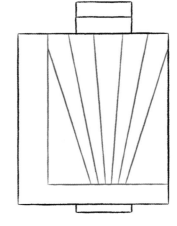

Diagram 5

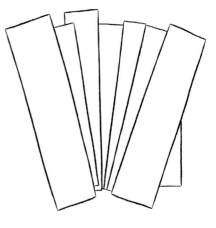

Diagram 6

Constructing your quilt

If a layout diagram is given, be sure to refer to it as well as to the quilt photograph. Many quilt designs, especially complex ones using more than one type of block, feature optical illusions caused by the way in which the various components are combined. Sometimes the logic of the quilt's construction will not become clear until you look at a layout diagram.

Adding borders

Borders may be added for decorative effect or to increase the quilt's size, or both. The corners may be either squared-off or mitered, but all of the borders in this book's projects have squared-off corners. The quilt pattern will tell you what length to cut the borders, but you should always measure your quilt before cutting the border fabric, and then adjust the length of the border strips if necessary.

Measure in both directions through the middle of the quilt rather than along the edges. This is because the edges may have distorted a little during the making of the quilt, especially if any of the edge pieces are bias cut. Use these measurements to calculate the length of each border.

Squared-off borders

If you are adding squared-off borders, the side borders will be the length of the quilt top, while the top and bottom borders will be the width of the quilt top with the side borders added. Unless a pattern indicates otherwise, sew the side borders on first, press the seams toward the border, and then add the top and bottom borders.

Layering the quilt

Once you have added all the borders, and before you can begin quilting, you need to assemble all three layers of the quilt (see Diagram 7).

The batting (wadding) and backing fabric should both be at least 4 in. (10 cm) larger all around than the quilt top. Press the quilt top and backing fabric. Lay the backing fabric right side down on a large, flat, clean surface (preferably one that is not carpeted), smooth it out carefully and then tape it to the surface using masking tape. Tape it at intervals along

all sides, but do not tape the corners, as this will cause the bias to stretch out of shape.

Place the batting on top of the backing fabric and smooth it out. Center the well-pressed quilt top, right side up, on top of the batting, ensuring that the top and backing are square to each other. Smooth out.

Types of batting (wadding)

Some battings (waddings) need to be quilted closer together than others to stop them from drifting around within the quilt or fragmenting when the quilt is washed. Polyester batting requires less quilting than cotton or wool batting. However, some polyester battings have a tendency to "fight" the sewing machine.

Wool battings (usually actually a wool/polyester or a wool/cotton blend) provide more warmth and comfort than polyester battings. However, they require more quilting, and those that are not needle-punched tend to pill. Needle-punched wool blends are more stable and require less quilting. Traditional cotton battings require a lot of quilting—as much as every ½ in. (1.2 cm). Needle-punched cotton

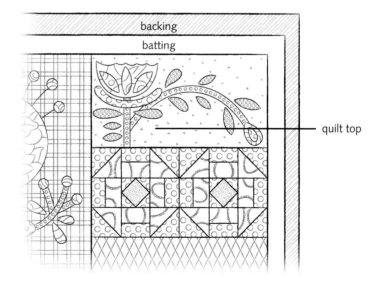

Diagram 7

battings are more stable and can be quilted up to 10 in. (25.5 cm) apart. Ask your quilt store for advice if you are unsure of what to choose.

As dolly quilts are so small and will be used only for display, it is perfectly acceptable to use offcuts of any kind of batting you have around. The ends that have been trimmed from a larger quilt are ideal.

Basting (tacking)

Once you have assembled the three layers, you need to baste (tack) them together ready for quilting. Basting can be done with safety pins (when machine quilting) or long hand stitches (when hand quilting).

If you are using safety pins, prior to machine quilting, start from the center of the quilt and pin through all three layers at intervals of about 8 in. (20.5 cm). Make sure the pins are kept away from the lines to be quilted. Once the whole quilt is safety-pinned, it can be moved. Do not use safety pins if you are hand quilting, as the pins prevent the hoop from sitting evenly.

To baste using hand stitches, prior to hand quilting, baste the whole quilt both horizontally and vertically, always working from the center out, using long hand stitches at intervals of about 5 in. (12.5 cm). Using a curved needle is a good idea, as this makes the task easier on the wrists. Do not baste using hand stitches if you intend to machine quilt, as the basting threads will get caught under the presser foot.

Some quilting stores offer a machine-basting service. This can be a worthwhile investment, especially if you are going to be hand quilting in the traditional manner, a task that can take months or even years for a large quilt. Remove the safety pins or basting stitches only after all the quilting is complete.

Quilting

The quilting can be fairly rudimentary, its main purpose being to hold together the layers of the quilt, or it can be decorative and sometimes extremely elaborate. Machine quilting is quicker, but nothing beats hand quilting for sheer heirloom beauty and a soft hand to the finished quilt.

Designs for hand quilting, or elaborate designs for domestic machine quilting, are generally marked on the quilt top before the quilt's layers are sandwiched together. On pale fabrics, the marking is done lightly in pencil; on dark fabrics, a special quilter's silver pencil is used. Pencil lines can be erased later.

If you intend to quilt straight lines or a crosshatched design, masking tape can be used to mark out the lines on the quilt top. Such tape comes in various widths, from ¼ in. (6 mm) upward. Free-flowing lines can be drawn on with a chalk pencil. If you intend to outline-quilt by machine, you may be able to sew straight-enough lines by eye; if not, you will need to mark the quilt top first.

Hand quilting

Quilting by hand produces a softer line than machine quilting and will emphasize the lovingly handmade quality of the quilt. Many of the quilts in this book are quilted using perle cotton, since it is often easier for beginners to work with and stands out vividly against the fabric's surface, although traditional waxed quilting thread can be used if you prefer.

To quilt by hand, the fabric needs to be held in a frame (also known as a quilting hoop). Freestanding frames are available, but hand-held ones are cheaper, more portable, and just as effective. One edge of a hand-held frame can be rested against a table or bench to enable you to keep both hands free.

Hand quilting, like machine quilting, should commence in the center of the quilt and proceed outward. To commence hand quilting, place the plain (inner) ring of the frame under the center of the quilt. Position the other ring, with the screw, over the top of the quilt to align with the inner ring. Tighten the screw so that the fabric in the frame becomes firm, but not drum-tight.

For traditional quilting, choose the smallest needle that you feel comfortable with. (These needles are known as "betweens.") For quilting with perle cotton, use a good-quality crewel embroidery needle. Sarah prefers a no. 9, but a 10 or 11 may be more comfortable for you.

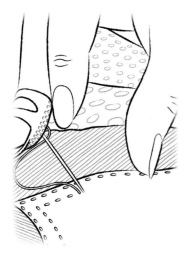

Diagram 8

Diagram 9

Diagram 10

1 Thread the needle with about 18 in. (45.5 cm) of thread. Knot the end of the thread with a one-loop knot and take the needle down through the quilt top into the batting (wadding), a short distance from where you want to start quilting. Tug the thread slightly so that the knot pulls through the fabric into the batting, making the starting point invisible.

2 With your dominant hand above the quilt and the other beneath, insert the needle through all three layers at a time with the middle or index finger of your dominant hand (use a metal thimble to make this easier) until you can feel the tip of the needle resting on your finger at the back (see Diagram 8).

3 Without pushing the needle through, rock the needle back to the top of the quilt and use your underneath finger to push the tip of the needle up. Put your upper thumb down in front of the needle tip while pushing up from the back (see Diagram 9). This will make a small "hill" in the fabric.

4 Push the needle through the hill. This makes one stitch. To take several stitches at once, push the needle along to the required stitch length, then dip the tip into the fabric and repeat the above technique (see Diagram 10). Gently pull the stitches to indent the stitch line evenly. You should always quilt toward yourself, as this reduces hand and shoulder strain, so turn the quilt in the required direction.

You can protect your underneath finger using a self-adhesive finger pad such as a Thimble-It. Or you can use a leather thimble, although this does make it more difficult to feel how far the needle has come through, and thus more difficult to keep your stitches neat and even.

5 To finish, hold the thread out to the side with your left hand, and loop a one-loop knot using the needle (see Diagram 11).

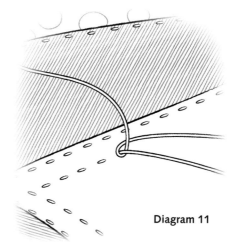

Diagram 11

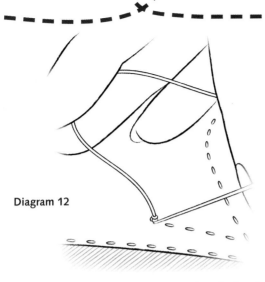

Diagram 12

6 Slide the loose knot down the thread until it lies directly on the quilt top, and tighten the knot. Take the needle back down through the hole the thread is coming out of and slide it away through the batting (see Diagram 12). Bring the needle back up to the top of the quilt and give the thread a tug. The knot will follow down into the hole and lodge in the batting. Cut the thread close to the surface. (To see a video tutorial of this technique, see the sidebar of Sarah's blog, www.thelastpiece.net.)

Machine quilting

Match the machine quilting thread to your needle size, to help avoid skipped and broken stitches. For smaller quilts, a standard 50 weight sewing thread should be fine, as there is no need for a stronger thread. A thicker quilting thread could also overpower a smaller design but your taste can dictate this choice. A sharps needle is a good choice but needle suitability can vary from machine to machine.

When you have finished machine quilting, pull the thread ends to the back, tie, and cut off the excess.

Straight-line quilting

For straight-line machine quilting, you will need a walking foot on the sewing machine. This foot feeds the fabric from the top while the feed dogs feed the fabric from below. Because the layers will be moving evenly, it will prevent the layers of the quilt from bunching up. Straight-line quilting can be done "in the ditch" along seams or in an even grid across the quilt top.

Free-motion quilting

For free-motion quilting, you will need to use a darning foot, which has a small circle of metal at its base. You will also need to be able to drop the feed dogs on the sewing machine. This disengages them so that you are guiding the fabric through the machine with your hands.

Think of the sewing machine needle as a pen and the layered quilt as the paper below it, but where you write by moving the paper rather than the pen. Move the layered quilt around with your fingertips in a steady manner to get gentle curves. Using the foot pedal, adjust the speed to your steady hand movements to get an even stitch length. Moving your hands too fast will result in forming stitch "eyelashes" when going around curves. Moving the quilt steadily and evenly is the key. Note that we didn't say "slow." Sometimes going faster is better so that you get a feel for obtaining even stitches.

Amy used free-motion quilting in a double teardrop pattern (see Diagram 13) on Candy is Dandy (see page 16) and Pretty Little Half Hex (see page 40), and an all-over swirl motif (see Diagram 14) on Fans of May (see page 70).

Diagram 13

Diagram 14

Binding

The binding is the narrow strip of folded fabric that wraps around the outer edges of the quilt to hide the raw edges of the quilt top, batting (wadding), and backing. Binding strips can be straight-cut (at right angles to the selvages) when used to bind straight edges, but if there are curved edges or curved corners, the strips must be cut on the bias.

You will need to cut enough strips for the total length to equal the outside edge of the quilt, plus about 6 in. (15 cm) to allow for mitered corners and for the ends to be folded under. For the double-thickness method shown here, the width of the strips needs to be at least six times the width of the binding you want to see from the right side. Amy and Sarah like this exposed part of the binding to be ¼ in. (6 mm) wide, so the strips need to be at least 1½ in. (4 cm) wide. Amy actually cuts her binding strips 2¼ in. (6 cm) wide and Sarah cuts hers 3 in. (7.5 cm) wide, but they look the same from the front because the extra binding is at the back of the quilt.

Straight-cut binding

1 Trim the backing and the batting so that they are even with the edge of the quilt top. Cut the strips from the width of the binding fabric.

2 To join the strips into a continuous length, fold under one end of one strip at a 45-degree angle and finger-press a crease. Unfold. The crease line will become the seam line. Mark this line lightly with a pencil. With right sides together and the two fabric pieces at 90 degrees, align the angled cut end with the next strip of binding fabric. Align the ¼ in. (6 mm) measurement on a quilter's ruler with this line and trim off the corner. Sew the two strips together along the marked line. Press all seams to one side and trim off the "ears" (see Diagram 15).

3 Press the entire strip in half along its length, with wrong sides together (see Diagram 16). Doubling the fabric like this makes the binding more durable.

4 Beginning at one end of the binding strip, pin the binding to the right side of the quilt along one edge, starting about 4 in. (10 cm) from a corner and aligning the raw edges.

Attach a walking foot to the machine and sew the binding in place through all layers along the first edge, using a ¼ in. (6 mm) seam allowance, but leaving the first 1 in. (2.5 cm) of the binding unstitched.

5 When you reach the corner, you will need to miter the binding, so end the seam ¼ in. (6 mm) from the corner and fasten off. Fold the remaining binding up at a 45-degree angle and then fold it down so that the fold is level with the edge of the binding you have just sewn. Begin the next seam at the edge of the quilt and proceed as before.

6 Repeat steps 4 and 5 until you are approaching the point at which the binding started. Trim the excess, turn back the end of the binding using a diagonal fold, and tuck this end under the starting end. Now stitch the rest of the seam.

7 Press the binding away from the quilt. Turn the binding to the back of the quilt, covering the seam line on the back, and blind hemstitch in place by hand.

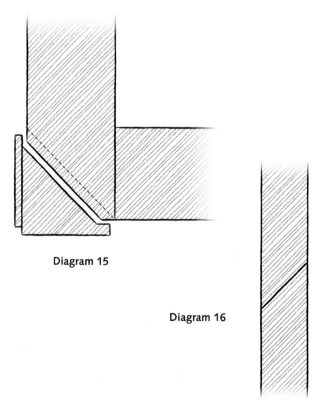

Diagram 15

Diagram 16

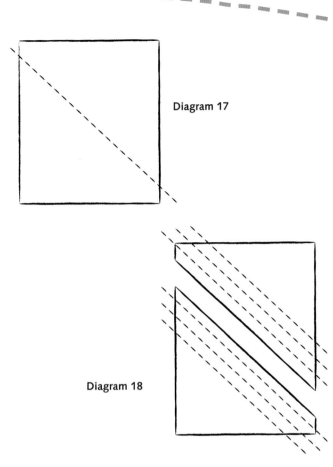

Diagram 17

Diagram 18

Bias binding

1 Bias binding for the small quilts in this book can be cut from fat quarters of fabric. Begin by cutting through the center of a fat quarter at a 45-degree angle (see Diagram 17).

2 Cut strips the required width along the bias edges of the two triangles cut from the fat quarter (see Diagram 18). Join the binding strips on the diagonal as described in step 2 for straight-cut binding.

3 Fold the bias binding in half and attach it as for straight-cut binding, steps 3–7 but taking care to gently guide the bias binding around the curved edge without stretching.

Adding a label

Once you have finished your quilt, add a label so that future generations know who made it, especially if the quilt is a gift. You can buy preprinted fabric labels, or simply write on a piece of coordinating fabric with a laundry marker, and slipstitch it to the back of the quilt. Add the year of making too.

Templates

All templates in this book are shown at 100%, so there is no need to enlarge them. They can simply be photocopied or traced.

What a Star

(See pages 10–15)

What a Star Template A
(Seam allowance included)

What a Star Template B
(Seam allowance included)

What a Star Template C
(Seam allowance included)

Not Quite Hawaiian

(See pages 36–39)
Motif Template
(Add seam allowance to fabric)

Polka-dot Baskets

(See pages 30–35)

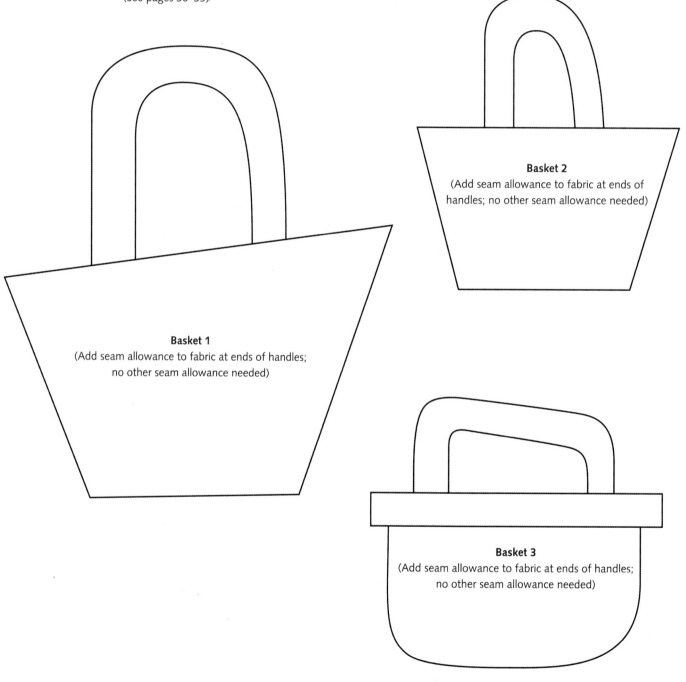

Basket 1
(Add seam allowance to fabric at ends of handles;
no other seam allowance needed)

Basket 2
(Add seam allowance to fabric at ends of
handles; no other seam allowance needed)

Basket 3
(Add seam allowance to fabric at ends of handles;
no other seam allowance needed)

Basket 5
(Add seam allowance to fabric at ends of handles;
no other seam allowance needed)

Basket 4
(Add seam allowance to fabric at ends of handles;
no other seam allowance needed)

Basket 6
(Add seam allowance to fabric at
ends of handles; no other seam
allowance needed)

Apple Orchard

(See pages 48–53)

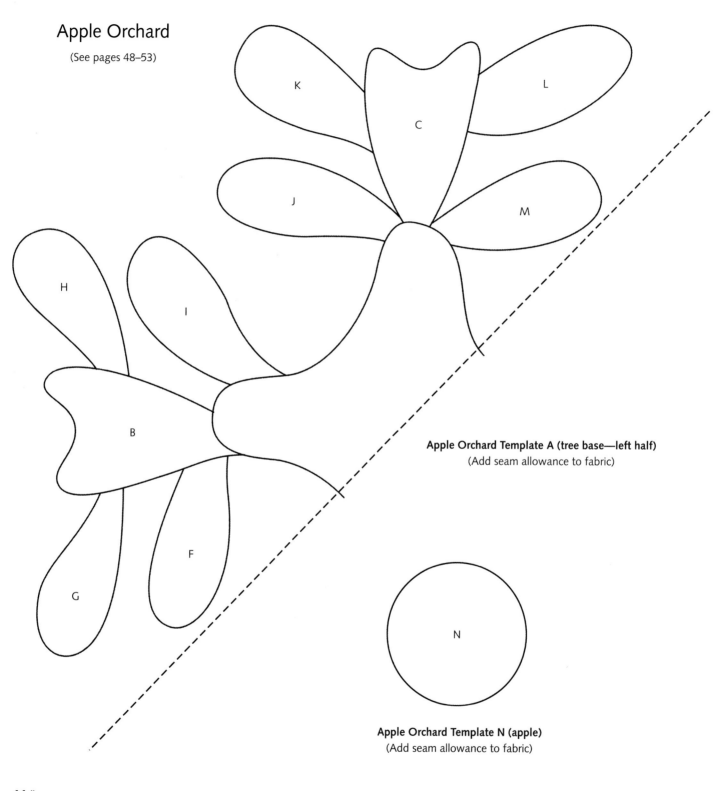

K

C

L

J

M

H

I

B

Apple Orchard Template A (tree base—left half)
(Add seam allowance to fabric)

F

G

N

Apple Orchard Template N (apple)
(Add seam allowance to fabric)

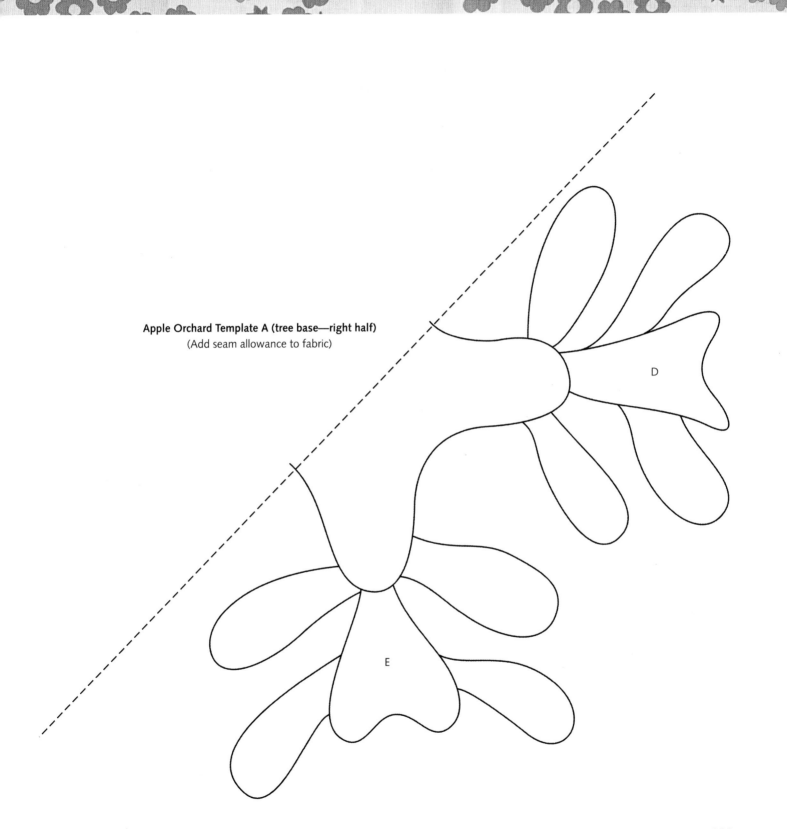

Apple Orchard Template A (tree base—right half)
(Add seam allowance to fabric)

D

E

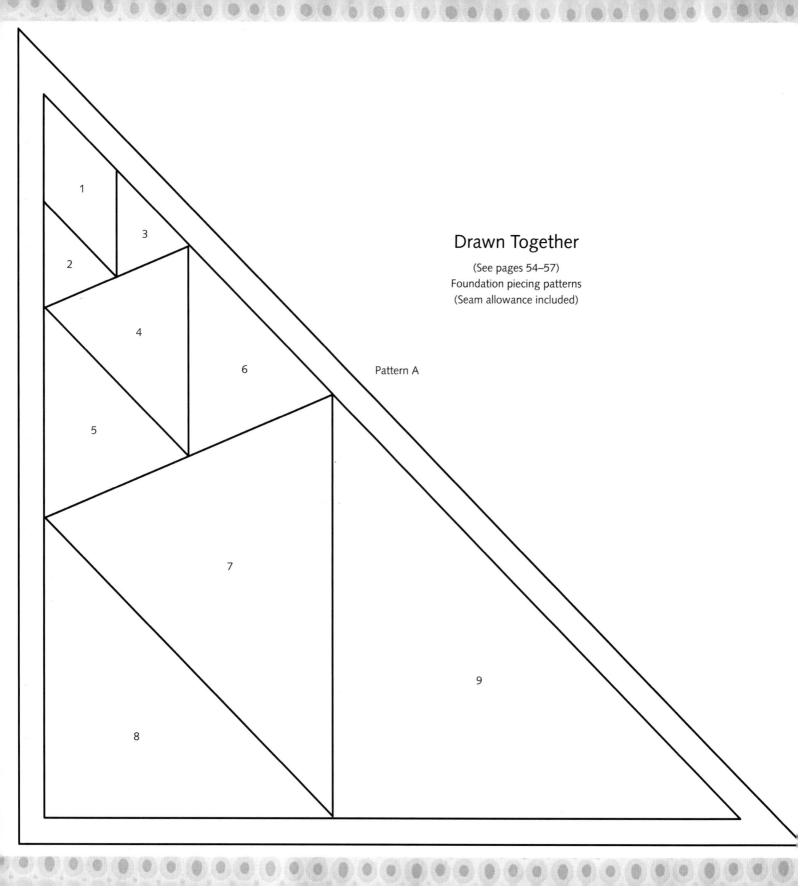

Drawn Together

(See pages 54–57)
Foundation piecing patterns
(Seam allowance included)

Pattern A

1

2

3

4

5

6

7

8

9

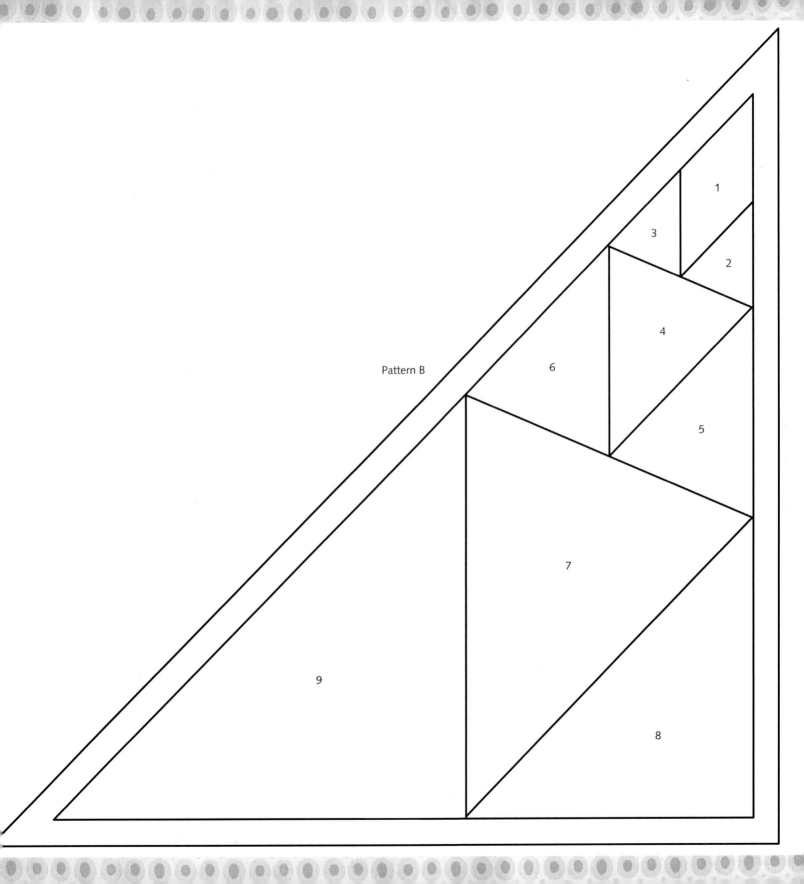

Pattern B

Pretty Little Half Hex

(See pages 40–43)

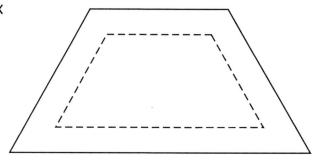

Pretty Little Half Hex Template
(Seam allowance included)

My Heart

(See pages 44–47)

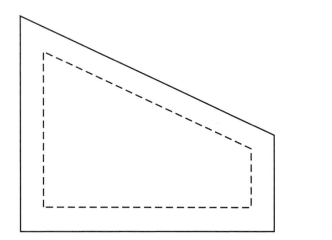

My Heart Template A (windmill)
(Seam allowance included)

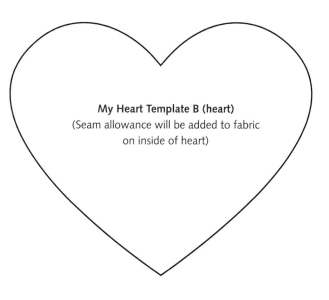

My Heart Template B (heart)
(Seam allowance will be added to fabric
on inside of heart)

Cocktail Shakers

(See pages 58–63)

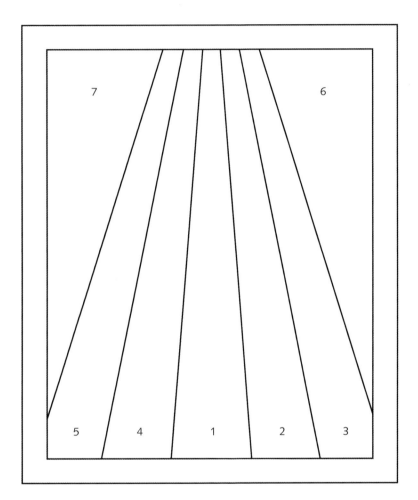

Foundation piecing pattern
(Seam allowance included)

Fans of May

(See pages 70–77)

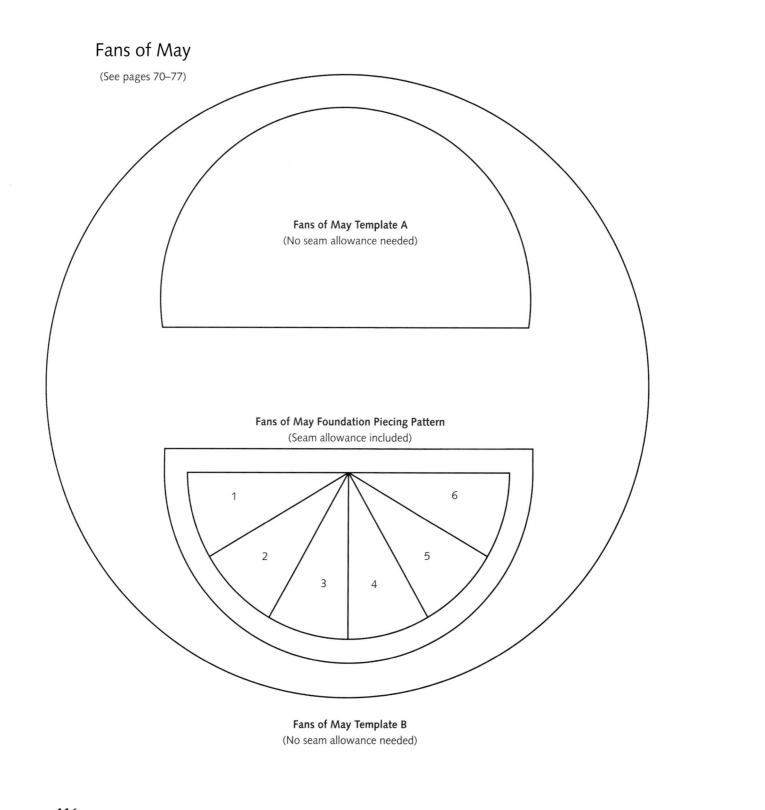

Fans of May Template A
(No seam allowance needed)

Fans of May Foundation Piecing Pattern
(Seam allowance included)

1

2

3   4

5

6

Fans of May Template B
(No seam allowance needed)

Honeycomb
(See pages 78–83)

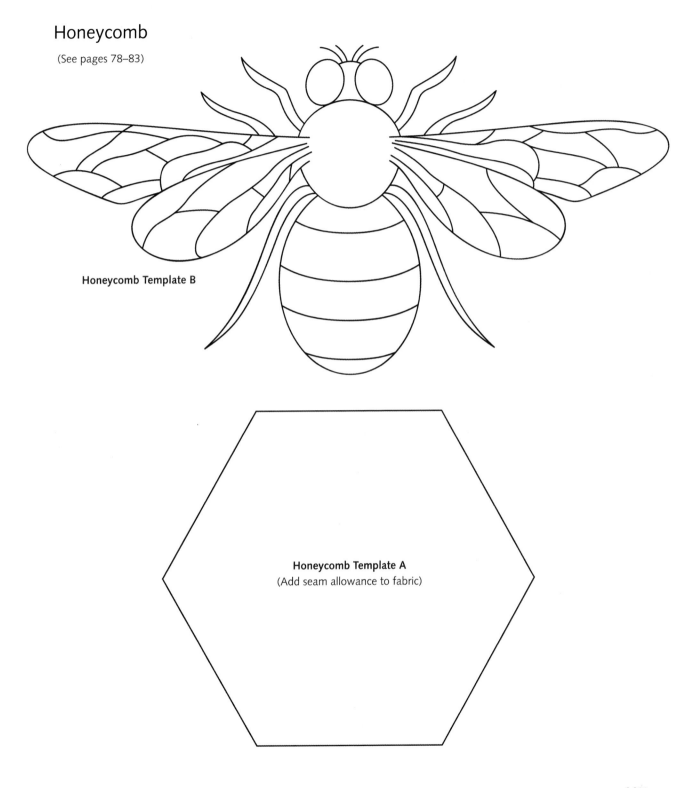

Honeycomb Template B

Honeycomb Template A
(Add seam allowance to fabric)

Paper Dolls

(See pages 84–89)

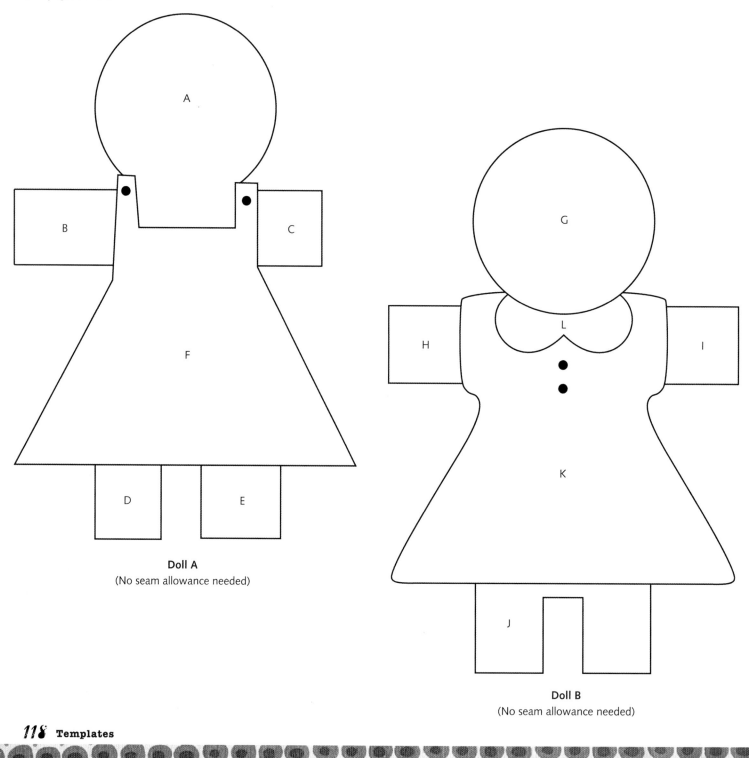

Doll A
(No seam allowance needed)

Doll B
(No seam allowance needed)

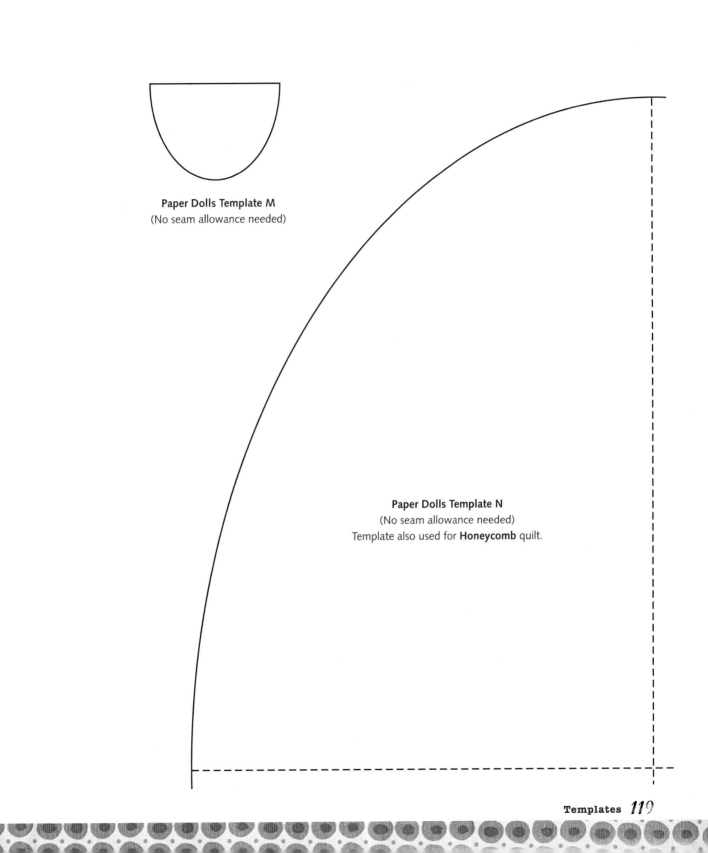

Paper Dolls Template M
(No seam allowance needed)

Paper Dolls Template N
(No seam allowance needed)
Template also used for **Honeycomb** quilt.

Cuttings

(See pages 90–95)

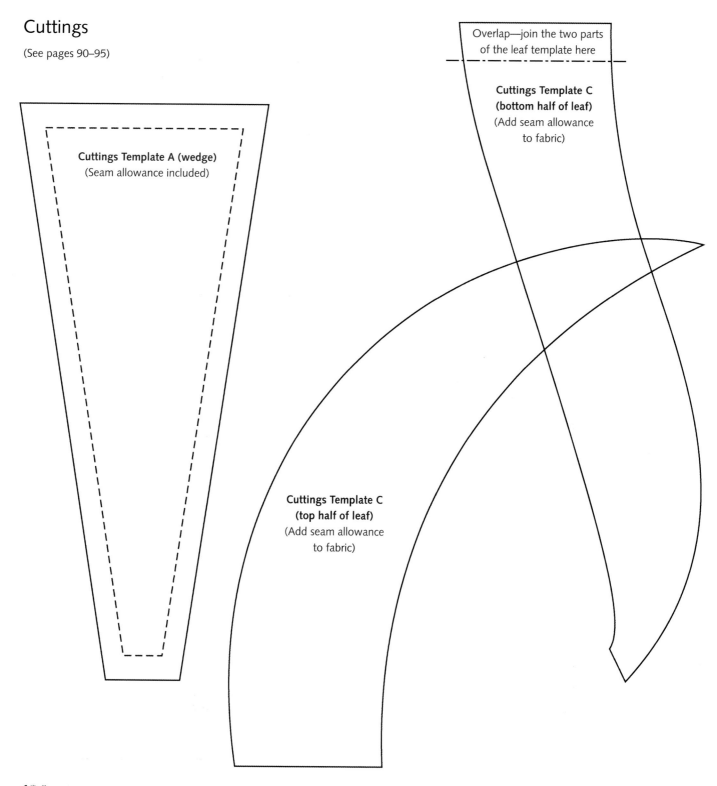

Cuttings Template A (wedge)
(Seam allowance included)

Overlap—join the two parts
of the leaf template here

Cuttings Template C
(bottom half of leaf)
(Add seam allowance
to fabric)

Cuttings Template C
(top half of leaf)
(Add seam allowance
to fabric)

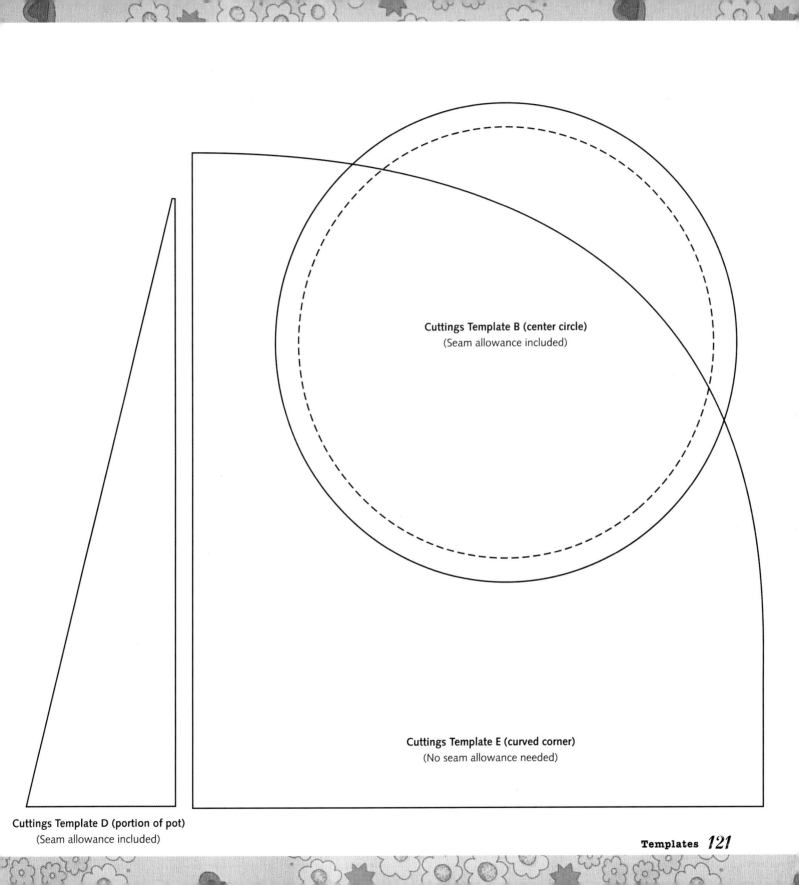

Cuttings Template B (center circle)
(Seam allowance included)

Cuttings Template E (curved corner)
(No seam allowance needed)

Cuttings Template D (portion of pot)
(Seam allowance included)

Glossary

Appliqué

A technique in which small pieces of fabric are stitched to a background fabric.

Backing

The undermost layer of a quilt.

Basting (tacking)

A method of holding together several layers of fabric during quilting, so that they do not move around. Basting may be done using a long hand stitch, or with safety pins. The stitches or pins are removed once the quilting is complete.

Batting (wadding)

The middle layer of a quilt; also known as wadding.

Bias

The diagonal of a woven fabric, at a 45-degree angle to the straight grain (the warp and weft). Fabric cut on the bias stretches, so care must be taken when handling and sewing bias-cut pieces. Compare with "grain."

Binding

The narrow strips of fabric (usually made of a double thickness) that enclose the raw edges and batting of a quilt.

Block

The basic unit of a patchwork quilt top. Blocks are usually square, but may be rectangular, hexagonal, or other shapes. They may be plain (of one fabric only), appliquéd, or pieced.

Border

A strip of fabric (plain, appliquéd, or pieced) joined to the central panel of a quilt and used to frame it and also to add extra size.

Crosshatching

A quilting pattern of parallel equidistant lines that run in two directions to form a grid of squares or diamonds.

Ease

To make two pieces of fabric of different sizes fit together in the one seam. One piece may have to be stretched or gathered slightly to bring it to the required length. To ease, first pin the pieces at intervals until they fit, then sew them.

English paper piecing

A technique that involves hand piecing shapes of fabric that are basted onto paper templates and then joined with whipstitches on the fabric edges.

Fat quarter

A piece of fabric that is made by cutting a meter or a yard of fabric in halves first vertically then horizontally. The piece thus cut is approximately 18 x 22 in. (50 x 56 cm).

Feed dogs

The teeth under the sewing plate of a sewing machine, which move to pull the fabric through the machine. The feed dogs must be lowered to allow for free-motion quilting.

Finger-pressing

A way of pressing a temporary crease in a piece of fabric, for example when finding the middle of two pieces so that they can be matched before being joined. Running a fingernail along a crease will make it lie flat.

Foundation piecing

Piecing using a paper foundation for stabilization and accuracy.

Fusible web

A lacy-like iron-on glue that comes with a paper backing.

Fussy cut

To cut out a pieced shape centered on a printed motif on the fabric, rather than cutting it out at random.

Grain

The direction of the fabric, along the warp (vertical threads) or the weft (horizontal threads). These are both straight grains, along which woven fabrics do not stretch. Compare with "bias."

Half-square triangle

A triangle that is made from a square, cut across one diagonal. Half-square triangles have the bias along the hypotenuse (or longest side). Compare with "quarter-square triangle."

Hexagon

A polygon shape with six sides.

Mitered corner

A corner that is joined at a 45-degree angle.

Novelty print

A fabric printed with themed designs, such as toys, cartoon characters, or animals.

On point

An arrangement in which the quilt blocks are placed diamond fashion, with their corners at the 12, 3, 6, and 9 o'clock positions, rather than in a square fashion.

Outline-quilt

To make one or more outlines of a motif or block design, radiating outward.

Patchwork

A generic term for the process of sewing together many small pieces of fabric to make a quilt; also known as piecework.

Piece

An individual fabric shape that may be joined to other fabric shapes to make a quilt block, or used on its own (in which case it is known as a one-patch). Also known as a patch.

Piecing

The process of joining together pieces of fabric to make a quilt top, a quilt block, or a border.

Pin-baste

To pin through the layers of a quilt "sandwich," using safety pins, to hold them together during quilting. The pins are removed once the quilting is complete.

Quarter-square triangle

A triangle that is made from a square, cut across both diagonals. Quarter-square triangles have the bias along the two short sides. Compare with "half-square triangle."

Quilt top

The uppermost, decorative layer of a quilt. It may be pieced, appliquéd, or a combination of both, with or without borders.

Quilter's ruler

Precision-cut, straight-edged plastic rulers in various sizes, used with rotary cutters and rotary-cutting (self-healing) mats. They make it easy to cut accurate shapes and to cut through several layers of fabric at once. They come in straight varieties and also those designed for cutting at various angles or for creating triangles.

Quilting

In general, the process of making a quilt; more specifically, the process of stitching patterns by hand or machine through the quilt layers to decorate the quilt, add strength, and anchor the batting (wadding) inside the quilt.

Quilting frame

A free-standing floor apparatus made of wood or plastic tubing, in which a quilt is held while it is being quilted.

Quilting hoop

A hand-held circular wooden device in which a quilt is held while being quilted.

Raw edge

The cut edge of a fabric.

Rickrack

Braided trimming in a zigzag pattern.

Rotary cutter

A cutting device similar in appearance to a pizza cutter, with a razor-sharp circular blade. Used in conjunction with a quilter's ruler and rotary cutting mat, it allows several layers of fabric to be cut at once, easily and with great accuracy.

Rotary-cutting mat

A self-healing plastic mat on which rotary cutters are used. It protects both the blade of the cutter and the work surface beneath the mat during cutting.

Sashing

Strips of fabric that separate blocks in a quilt, to frame them and/or make the quilt larger.

Seam allowance

The margin of fabric between the cut edge and seam line. For quilting and most appliqué, it is ¼ in. (6 mm).

Seam line

The guideline that is followed while sewing.

Selvages (selvedges)

The woven finished edges along the length of the fabric.

Setting

The way in which blocks are arranged in a quilt top, for example, square or on point.

Setting square

A plain block or square used with pieced or appliquéd blocks in a quilt top.

Setting triangle

A triangle placed between blocks along the sides of a quilt set on point, to straighten up the edges.

Stash

A quilter's hoard of fabrics.

Tacking

See "basting."

Template

Plastic, card, or paper shape used for tracing and cutting fabric pieces for piecing or appliqué or to transfer quilting designs to a quilt top.

Wadding

See "batting."

Walking foot

A special sewing machine foot that feeds the top layer of a quilt sandwich evenly through the machine, while the feed dogs control the bottom layer.

Warp

The lengthwise threads in a woven fabric, which interlock with the weft threads; see also "weft."

Weft

The widthwise threads in a woven fabric, which interlock with the warp threads; see also "warp."

"Y" seam

Where three seams come together at one intersection and all of them must start from the same place.

Resources

We're aware that many people who buy this book may be just starting out on their quilting journeys. Here are a few interesting places to go, and websites for shopping.

There are many wonderful bricks-and-mortar quilt shops in the world and, where possible, we encourage you to shop at your local patchwork shop rather than buy online. We know this isn't always possible but, while no quilt shop can stock everything, staff at your local store will help you select your fabric, give you recommendations and hints, and offer great workshops to help develop your skills. Your local quilt store can't stay in business to run classes unless you also shop with them. Support your local quilt shop!

Obviously, listing every quilt shop here is not possible, so here are a few online shops we like to visit (and they ship worldwide).

Fabric online

Fabricworm www.fabricworm.com

Glorious Color www.gloriouscolor.com

Pink Castle Fabrics www.pinkcastlefabrics.com

Sew Mama Sew www.sewmamasew.com

Westwood Acres www.westwoodacresfabric.com

Pink Chalk Fabrics www.pinkchalkfabrics.com

Notions (haberdashery) online

These are the brands we prefer at the moment:

For piecing
Aurifil Cotton 12 thread

For appliqué
Patchwork with Busyfingers size 11 milliners needles

Aurifil Cotton 50 thread

Patchwork with Busyfingers appliqué glue

An appliqué kit is available from Sarah's website.

For quilting
John James Pebble size 10 crewel embroidery needles

Presencia Finca perle 8 and perle 12 cotton thread

Clover open-sided thimble

Bonwick quilting hoop

Matilda's Own 100 percent cotton batting (wadding)

Quilter's Dream 100 percent cotton batting (wadding)

Perspex template sets

We have perspex template sets available for purchase for these quilts:

Cuttings
Fans of May
Garden Paths
Honeycomb
My Heart
Pretty Little Half Hex
What a Star

Visit www.sarahfielke.com for details and, yes, we ship worldwide.

Sarah and Amy have developed a range of patterns for large quilts using the dolly quilt patterns. They are available from www.sarahfielke.com.

Resources for information and online classes

Generation Q Magazine www.generationqmagazine.com

Craftsy www.craftsy.com

Fat Quarterly www.fatquarterly.com

Join a Quilt Guild near you—you will meet other quilters and be inspired by their work and enriched by their company. Sarah is a member of The Quilters' Guild of NSW Inc. and the Greater Western Sydney Modern Quilt Guild.

Inspirational blogs for quilts, fabrics, and fun

Bemused www.bemused.typepad.com

I'm a Ginger Monkey www.imagingermonkey.blogspot.com

Pam Kitty Morning www.pamkittymorning.blogspot.com

Piece and Press www.pieceandpress.blogspot.com

Red Pepper Quilts www.redpepperquilts.com

The Happy Zombie www.thehappyzombie.com

You Patch www.youpatch.com

Poppy Print Creates www.poppyprintcreates.blogspot.com

Find us online

We love hearing from you and answering questions if you have made our quilts or enjoyed our book. Come and say hi!

Sarah

Website: www.sarahfielke.com

Blog: www.thelastpiece.net

Email: sarah@sarahfielke.com

Twitter: @sarahfielke

Facebook: /sarah.fielke

Pinterest: sarahfielke

Instagram: @sfielke

Flickr: sfielke

Sarah teaches regular classes in Sydney, and she often teaches interstate and overseas. She teaches online classes at Craftsy.com. You can find details of her latest classes on her blog, or send her an email to ask for a class list if you would like her to visit your local shop or group.

Sarah's latest fabric ranges for Spotlight Australia are available through Spotlight stores in Australia, New Zealand, and Singapore or from her website. Her latest fabric range for Windham Fabrics is available from patchwork stores. Her range of appliqué threads for Aurifil Threads is available from patchwork stores and from Sarah's website.

Amy

Blog:
www.mrsschmenkmanquilts.wordpress.com

Email: alobsiger@gmail.com

Twitter: @alobsiger

Facebook: /alobsiger

Instagram: @alobsiger

Pinterest: alobsiger

Flickr: alobsiger

Amy works at her local quilt shop, but can be persuaded to teach or make you a quilt.

Index

Acknowledgments

From Sarah:

Thank you to the wonderful team at CICO Books: to Cindy Richards for her continuing faith in my projects, to Gillian Haslam for her level-headed management, and to Sally Powell for the beautiful design.

Thank you in buckets to my marvelous friend Sue Stubbs for her good-enough-to-eat photography and her pre-shoot chats.

Thank you to Erica Spinks for her confident editing, her friendship, and her steadfast support. Good to have you on board, lovely!

To Amy, the only person with whom I would ever write another book. The only flaw in our friendship is that you are too far away!

Thank you to all the quilters, near and far, who read my books and blogs, buy my fabric, and take my classes. You are all just the bomb.

Most especially, thank you to my long-suffering, living-in-a-messy-house, surrounded-by-quilts, and buried-under-fabric husband and boys. There isn't anything more important than you guys. Yes, that does include the fabric!

From Amy:

For Dan who made things seem possible. For Anabel who keeps me going.

Thank you to Joe who brought new joy to life. I still don't think he knows what he's in for.

My heartfelt thank you to Sarah for all of this, for friendship, for sarcasm, for inspiration, for helping me to laugh even in the grimmest moments. Were it not for her, I wouldn't be writing this right now. Thank you.

Thanks to the wonderful team at CICO Books for letting me join in the fun with my pal: Cindy Richards, Gillian Haslam, and Sally Powell. Thanks to Sue Stubbs for the loveliest of photos. Thanks to Erica Spinks for fantastically wise editing.

Thank you to Anastasia, Cathy, Jennifer, and Susan for wine, coffee, love, and sanity.

Thanks to Nanci and all of my wonderful co-workers at Guildcrafters Quilt Shop.

Certainly not least, my thanks to quilters from around the world who sent me well wishes and buoyed me. The same goes to family and friends who have created an invisible net underneath my little family.

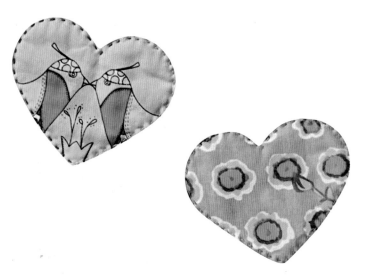